PRAISE FOR

DIVINE ECHOES

"Too often Christians fail to think theologically when they pray. That may seem odd because prayer is a profoundly theological activity. But Christians too often pray while simultaneously ignoring their theological questions, doubts, and past experiences. Mark Karris offers a compelling antidote: genuine theological reflection on what prayer is and why petitionary prayer doesn't always yield the results we seek. His proposals may shock you, but good medicine can sometimes do that. I highly recommend Mark's book!"

Thomas Jay Oord, author of 20+ books, including
The Uncontrolling Love of God

"Mark Karris begins this book with two heartbreaking stories of unanswered prayer from his own life. These stories set the stage for an honest and courageous rethinking of what it means to pray for others. He makes accessible some of the most important thinking going on in the theological community today about God's relationship to creation and the purposes of prayer. He will take you to a place where your prayers can be more honest, where God's love is completely trustworthy, and where you enter into a deep partnership with God."

Brian D. McLaren, author of *The Great Spiritual Migration*

"What an important work of spiritual guidance Karris is offering. No more begging and instructing God to do this or that—and suffering the endless disappointments! Instead, Karris teaches with his vividly inviting prose and wise theology an honestly loving and effectual 'conspiring prayer' practice for the benefit of the church and the world."

Catherine Keller, George T. Cobb Professor of
Constructive Theology, Drew Theological School, author
of *On the Mystery: Discerning God in Process*

"How many times do our prayers consist of throwing a bunch of requests against a proverbial wall and seeing what sticks? What happens when we pray for God to act in the world? In *Divine Echoes*, Mark Karris masterfully breaks down the myths and mechanisms of praying for divine *intervention*. Drawing on the idea of *essential kenosis*, Karris offers a model for petitionary prayer that is powered by the uncontrolling love of God and enacted through the libertarian free will given to humankind. Instead of merely praying *to* God and hoping that God acts, Karris enjoins the reader to pray *with* God, partnering with the good work God is already bringing about in the world."

R. Anderson Campbell, co-author of *Praying for
Justice: A Lectionary of Christian Concern*

"Mark Karris gives an important and practical lesson on prayer. He helps us combine healing engagement in our broken world with honesty about who God is and how God works in the world. He impressively merges deep theology and practice."

Ted Grimsrud, Senior Professor of Peace Theology, Eastern
Mennonite University, author of *Embodying the Way of Jesus*

"As a life-long intercessor who doesn't know how to pray (Rom. 8:26), I have nevertheless observed with Bishop Tutu that God does nothing in this world without a willing human partner. Mark Karris articulates this beautifully, developing a coherent theology and practice of petitionary prayer that honors the language of divine *kenosis* and human participation. He portrays and proclaims a caring, non-coercive God who loves the world through our agency."

Brad Jersak, author of *A More Christlike God: A More Beautiful Gospel*

"The personal and vulnerable stories shared, the compelling theological understanding of prayer presented, and a new and persuasive paradigm of petitionary prayer proposed makes this provocative book an invaluable work that belongs in everyone's library."

Grace Ji-Sun Kim, Associate Professor of Theology at Earlham School of Religion, author or editor of more than a dozen books, more recently, *Embracing the Other: The Transformative Spirit of Love*

"This is one of the best books on prayer I have ever read. It not only addresses the questions of why we should pray and what prayer is, but also the more important questions of how prayer works and how God works with us to see more of our prayers answered. After reading this book, you will stop praying *to* God and start conspiring *with* God and become the vital change we all desperately desire to see in the world."

J. D. Myers, author of *What is Prayer? How to Pray to God Like You Talk to a Friend*

"Mark Karris asks the hard questions about prayer that many of us are afraid to ask. By appealing to both Scripture and reason, he develops a new path forward and illustrates it with practical applications involving situations we all face. If you struggle with petitionary prayer, as I do, you should really consider Karris' approach, whether or not you end up adopting it as your own."

Scott A. Davison, Professor of Philosophy, Morehead State University, author of *Petitionary Prayer: A Philosophical Investigation*

"*Divine Echoes* is an excellent and thought-provoking treatise on the topic of petitionary prayer! It is movingly written, well-researched, filled with down-to-earth anecdotes and gentle argumentation. Mark Karris speaks to the curious mind and the hungry heart, helping us enter into a sacred activity that helps complete our humanity and bring forth health, healing, and wholeness to the world. Mark's proposed model of prayer, which he calls 'Conspiring Prayer', becomes an act of intimacy by which we grow closer to the Unity in whose loving presence we live and move and have our being. It also brings us closer to the people we already want to become: channels of loving grace in a broken but beautiful world."

Jay McDaniel, Professor of Religion, Hendrix College, author of *Replanting Ourselves in Beauty: Toward an Ecological Civilization*

"I am impressed with both the religious depth and the theological sophistication of this passionate interpretation of prayer. Many other readers will also find this a most helpful meditation on the meaning and power of petitionary prayer."

John F. Haught, distinguished research professor, Georgetown University, author of *Resting on the Future*

"In my work with people I've seen the harm caused by toxic and limited notions of prayer. Many are left wondering why their prayers went unanswered or feeling defeated because they apparently didn't have enough or the right kind of faith. As a therapist and theologian Mark Karris is uniquely equipped to help us navigate perplexing questions about prayer. *Divine Echoes* explores why we don't always get what we want and how disappointment can move us towards deeper intimacy and trust. If you are skeptical or have given up on petitionary prayer, this book might help you renew your practice and see prayer in a whole new way."

Mark Scandrette, author of *Belonging and Becoming* and *Practicing the Way of Jesus*

"Petitionary prayer is one of the Christian hard knots to untangle, for not only does it seem that petitionary prayers frequently go unanswered, but we presume that God can and should step in and unilaterally make things right. Karris, in a very readable and provocative book, helpfully challenges petitioners to be the very hands and feet of God in the world, implementing his loving concern for all."

Bruce R. Reichenbach, Professor Emeritus, Augsburg College, author of *Divine Providence: God's Love and Human Freedom*

"This is really a provocative and inspirational book!"

Bruce Epperly, author, or co-author, of over forty books, including *Praying with Process Theology: Spiritual Practices for Personal and Planetary Healing*

"*Divine Echoes* is an exceptionally fine reflection on the meaning of petitionary prayer. This book should find a warm reception in congregational study-groups, seminaries and divinity schools, as well as with anyone genuinely interested in pursuing a deeper understanding of prayer."

Owen F. Cummings, Academic Dean and Regents' Professor of Theology at Mount Angel Seminary, author of over eighteen publications, including *Thinking About Prayer*

"Most of us ignore or explain away the difficulties in Christian belief and practice. It is refreshing to find someone courageous and honest enough to investigate one such problem, that of the validity and purpose of prayer for others. Mark bases his work on personal experience and careful research and provides a valuable guide to how we can pray for others more properly and thus more effectively. This is a book which all thinking Christians should read!"

Christopher Huggett, BA, MPhil, PGCertEd., author of *A Theology of Becoming*

DIVINE ECHOES

RECONCILING PRAYER
WITH THE UNCONTROLLING
LOVE OF GOD

MARK GREGORY KARRIS

First Edition

Cover design and layout by Rafael Polendo (polendo.net)

All Scripture quotations, unless otherwise indicated, are from the Holy Bible, New International Version®, NIV®. Copyright © 1973, 1978, 1984, 2011 by Biblica, Inc.™ Used by permission of Zondervan. All rights reserved worldwide. www.zondervan.com.

Scripture quotations marked KJV are from the King James Version of the Bible. Scripture quotations marked NLT are from the New Living Translation Version of the Bible, *Holy Bible: New Living Translation*. Wheaton, IL: Tyndale House Publishers, 2004. Print. Scripture quotations marked NRSV are from the New Revised Standard Version of the Bible, copyright © 1989 by the National Council of the Churches of Christ in the U.S.A. Used by permission. All rights reserved.

"A Prayer for the Easter Vigil" adapted from *Coloring Lent: An Adult Coloring Book for the Journey to Resurrection* (St. Louis: CBP), 2017. (c) Christopher Rodkey, Jesse Turri, and Natalie Turri. Used by and adapted with permission of the authors. All rights reserved.

ISBN 978-1-938480-25-6

This volume is printed on acid free paper and meets ANSI Z39.48 standards.

Printed in the United States of America

Published by Quoir
Orange, California

www.quoir.com

ACKNOWLEDGMENTS

I am grateful for my village. Thank you to Samuel Kelly, Sarah Hussell, Ted Grimsrud, Chris Halls, Lee Warren, L. Michaels, Donna Fiser Ward, Luanne Austin, Cameron McCown, and my amazing wife Bianca for the helpful feedback, support, grammatical gracelets, and encouragement.

I would also like to thank Thomas J. Oord for his generous and courageous spirit. Your unwavering passion to see God's uncontrolling love blanket the earth is inspiring. It has, in fact, inspired the writing of this book.

I am dedicating this book to my precious son, Alexander. You are the reason I am so passionate about reimagining prayer. I want you to grow up in a world that is filled with more love, peace, grace, and beauty, or what we theologians call *shalom*. I hope this book contributes to that vision of love and harmony.

TABLE OF CONTENTS

INTRODUCTION

Every book has a backstory. Let me share a couple of events from my story, the seeds that brought this book to fruition.

I was six when my parents divorced. My siblings and I went to live with our mom. Our dad would pick us up on the weekends when he could. It was a constant, bitter feud between them, and, unfortunately, it is always the children who are affected the most. That was definitely the case for my siblings and me.

My mom was a smart, compassionate woman of strength. She did her best to raise us. Unfortunately, she was addicted to drugs as far back as I can remember. As you might imagine, that made it kind of hard to consistently love, protect, and take care of us. It is difficult to be emotionally attuned to your children when you are frantically trying to find out when and from where your next high is going to come. But she was my mom, the only one I had. I loved her and longed for her to be whole and well.

I became a Christian in my twenties. That is when I began praying fervently for my mother. Day after day, year after year, my heartfelt prayer was for God to save her and rid her of her debilitating addiction. Not only did *I* pray, but members of my church and other Christian friends also lifted her up in prayer on a regular basis. There were glimmering moments when I thought my mother had seen the light and had quit drugs, but those were fleeting. As the days and weeks went by, I grew tired of praying for her, but I never gave up. Then one day, the worst imaginable thing happened—she overdosed and died. I was devastated and heartbroken.

My mom wasn't the only family member for whom I was desperately praying. In our early years, my younger brother was one of the most loving, outgoing, creative, and intelligent people I knew. He was the life of the party, "the Man," as they say. He had tons of friends. Girls loved him. He was an amazing brother, friend, and fellow adventurer. That is, until the age of twenty-one, when something tragic happened that forever changed the course of his life and our lives as his family. I came home one day to find all my brother's belongings set outside at the curb. Of course, I found that very strange, so I went inside to ask him about it. What I found was my brother curled up in a ball, mumbling and incoherent. He had thrown out all of his belongings, but he had no idea why.

We soon learned that my brother was suffering a psychotic episode, the first of many. After that terrible day, he was never the same. My siblings and I were grief-stricken, having lost forever the loving, creative, intelligent brother we had known. Over the following days, my brother insisted that people were trying to kill him. At one point, he even declared himself to be Jesus Christ. In a grotesque parody of Christ's baptism, my brother baptized himself in a dirty, bug-infested lake not too far from our home. He believed this cleansed him from sin and he announced himself as the "savior of the world." It was so hard to watch knowing that he was the one who needed saving.

Eventually, the doctors diagnosed my brother with one of the cruelest forms of mental illness: paranoid schizophrenia. Along with his diagnosis came an endless cycle of psychotic episodes followed by hospitalizations and stabilizing medications. Just a few years ago, he stopped taking his medication, and his subsequent unstable behavior resulted in his incarceration. In prison, during a time when he was off his medication again, he murdered a fellow prisoner. He will never again set foot outside of prison walls.

Do you know how much I prayed for my brother over the years? A lot! So many others did too. In fact, years before he was incarcerated, the church I attended held deliverance services for him. We came together as a church, and even fasted beforehand, to pray relentlessly for my brother to be delivered from the demons we thought were tormenting him. When that didn't work, I took him to ministry personnel outside our own church who specialized in casting out demons. That didn't work either. My brother continued to unravel before our eyes. In time, I came to understand that his problem was not demon possession but an acute mental illness.

I tirelessly petitioned God on behalf of my brother. I cried, wailed, begged, and pleaded with him. My desire was for the all-powerful God of love and the Great Physician to heal my brother completely. I thought that if God would only snap his mighty fingers or whisper the word "healed," my brother's neuronal connections would fire properly again. Unfortunately, God never snapped his fingers or said a magic word. To this day, my brother remains tormented by one of the worst diseases of the mind an individual can have.

Well-known Christian philosopher Dallas Willard writes:

> The idea that everything would happen exactly as it does regardless of whether we pray or not is a specter that haunts the minds of many who sincerely profess belief in God. It makes prayer psychologically impossible, replacing it with dead ritual at best.[1]

The specter of the failure of prayer haunted me. I could not shake it. Something about it just did not add up. The tiresome steadfast Christian answers echoing from dear friends and mentors did not help at all. Constantly, I would hear things like:

- "God has a plan and is in control."
- "Your brother's healing is right around the corner."
- "If you fast and pray hard enough, God will give your brother a breakthrough."

Over time, those responses felt shallow and fell flat. The fate of my mother and brother, combined with the inadequacy of such clichés, set me on a mission to figure out the conundrum of prayer. Deep in my bones, I knew God's plan could not have included the deadly overdose that killed my mother. I also knew a slow, torturous, deathly, and dehumanizing existence inside a prison cell was not God's will or plan for my brother. I couldn't figure out how to rectify the existence of a good God with the lack of successful prayer for loved ones.

Even as I wrestled with these questions, I still participated in and benefited from personal prayer with God. I had read research studies that showed how time spent in individual prayer changes the brain and reduces stress and anxiety. I was also certain that face-to-face, ear-to-ear (praying together through technology), heart-to-heart, hands-on praying in community for others worked powerfully for those who could believe and were in their right mind.

But what about the many prayers we, as Christians, offer for people who are not only *not* face-to-face with us but who may not even know we are praying for them? And what about our prayers for those who may not have asked for, or even wanted, our prayers? What about our long-distance petitions for situations across town or across the world where there is a need for God's saving grace? Do such prayers make a difference? If so, how? And what determines which prayers are answered and which are not?

My own experience of unanswered prayers became a haunting ghost of doubt that impelled me to examine more closely just what petitionary prayer on behalf of others really entails. Years later, the doubts and questions I had reached a climax. As an ordained pastor and a licensed therapist who counseled countless others with similar questions, I realized the time was ripe for me to deconstruct and reimagine petitionary prayer. We have all heard such petitionary prayers:

- "God, heal my grandmother."
- "God, save my brother."
- "God, give the doctors wisdom."
- "God, please bring peace to that ravaged, war-torn nation."

Such beautiful pleas come from sincere hearts desperately praying for God to intervene in the lives of those they love. But does petitionary prayer offered on behalf of another, without the knowledge of that other person, effect any real change? Or do such prayers merely provide comfort for the one who is praying? Is there a way to pray more effectively to increase God's loving activity in the world while also reducing human and creaturely suffering? How does petitionary prayer for others work if those people have free will? If God is not "in control" of all things in the sense of dictating every action, reaction, or happening on this planet, how should that affect how we pray? These are questions I hope to address in this book.

In the chapters that follow, we shall travel from investigation to deconstruction to reconstruction of petitionary prayer offered on behalf of others. These prayers are differentiated from petitionary prayers being offered for oneself or for others while face-to-face or ear-to-ear. Praying for someone in person or over the phone allows that other person a choice at that moment to open up to God and submit to God's working in his or her life. The same goes for praying for oneself.

In contrast, those who are being prayed for at a distance, often without their knowledge or consent, may not be open to an experience from God. If they are open, there may be other variables to take into account when considering why praying for them may not be effective. Therefore, praying for others from a distance offers unique challenges that may not be present when praying for someone who is willing and consenting to the presence and grace of God.

For example, the types of petitionary prayers I explore include praying alone in one's room for a sick relative in another state or country and praying as individuals or communities for critical situations occurring on the other side of the planet that are in dire need of God's grace and intervention.

While examining petitionary prayers, we need to keep in mind what theologians call *theodicy*. Theodicy is the attempt to make sense of how a good, loving, and omnipotent God is involved, or not involved, with the harsh reality of evil and suffering in the world. In this book, I seriously posit one specific model of theodicy. It is called "essential kenosis," a model put forth by Thomas Jay Oord in his book, *The Uncontrolling Love of God: An Open and Relational Account of Providence.*[2] Many books address prayer, while others reflect on the topic of theodicy. In the following pages, our conversation will bring these two topics together.

Oord's approach centers on a few core propositions. First, he suggests that God's love is uncontrolling and non-coercive.[3] In other words, God doesn't force his way into people's lives because that would be contradictory to his nature. Therefore, evil exists to the extent that it does because a loving and uncontrolling God, by his very nature, cannot forcefully stop the people he has created from choosing to commit evil acts. Oord also states that God never intervenes in the world unilaterally;[4] he never acts alone, of his own accord, disregarding laws of nature and the free will of people. On the contrary, God always works through willing cooperation.[5]

Throughout this book, we will examine how these core propositions relate to petitionary prayer. We will also examine their implication and impact regarding issues of social justice. Theological certainties should be lived out in practical and liberating ways that benefit not only the church but also the world at large.

In the opening chapter, I will describe my initial journey into the topic of petitionary prayer. I have discovered the hard way that deconstructing a sacred practice as ancient and esteemed as petitionary prayer is no easy task. We will look at the blessings and difficulties surrounding issues of doubt, the questioning of faith, and the fear of rejection.

In chapter two, I will reflect upon the mysterious mechanics of prayer. In other words, my focus is on the question, "How does prayer work?" alongside other vital, challenging questions concerning petitionary prayer offered on behalf of others. These questions will serve as a starting point to expose areas of concern and potential pitfalls that we will discuss in chapter three.

In chapter three, we will examine various theological and philosophical concerns as they relate to petitionary prayer. One concern is that petitionary prayer has the potential to contribute, however unintentionally, to our doubts about the goodness of God. It can also lead us to neglect the reality of human free will. In other words, we can pray without taking into account that the person we are praying for can choose whether to accept or deny God's grace. We can also pray in a manner that distorts our image of God's loving character into one that is passive and cruel. Some prayers just make a good God look really bad.

In chapter four, we will briefly examine the science of petitionary prayer to determine its empirical validity and the extent to which it is effective in accomplishing what has been asked of God as some have claimed. To finish up this chapter, we will look at petitionary prayer within the context of experiential concerns, such as present-day evil, suffering, and social injustice. While petitionary prayer can be a loving and compassionate gesture, it can also become an obstacle to what God longs to accomplish in the world.

Chapter five explores petitionary prayer in the Bible. Here, we will use a deconstructive lens to examine verses commonly used to support petitionary prayer. I hope to shake loose some common petitionary prayer texts from their traditional explanations to propel us toward new pathways of theological thought and practice. I will also highlight certain concerns regarding the topic of theodicy and God's loving character. If our interpretation of a text portrays God in a manner contrary to that which we see in Jesus and to God's uncontrolling love, perhaps we need to reconsider how we interpret that text.

Chapter six will establish the theological and philosophical underpinnings for reimagining prayer as a more coherent, more effective practice than what is traditionally understood. We will explore God's character and manner of working in the world, establishing a love-infused theodicy based largely on Oord's essential kenosis, which prioritizes God's loving and uncontrolling nature.

Chapter seven continues on this theme by exploring what God's loving and uncontrolling nature means for how God interacts with human beings. We will ask what it means to be open to God and how and when God responds to our prayers. I will also define some of the limits of our knowledge in this area. We don't know all that God does, but we can seek integrity in the way we think about him.

In chapter eight, we will begin to construct a vision for a new way of practicing petitionary prayer that is mature and effective. I call this reimagined and subversive practice "conspiring prayer." This approach to petitionary prayer requires a paradigm shift that seeks to redefine petitionary prayer not as a monologue but as a dialogue. Put differently, petitionary prayer should move from simply praying *to* God to praying *with* God in order that shalom is brought forth to the world.

Chapter nine puts conspiring prayer into action. It is not enough to merely discuss theory and theology. An aching world demands sacred practices that have their feet on the ground, no matter how heavenly we deem their origin. We are called to be Divine Echoes—people who intentionally set aside time to prayerfully listen, humbly opening themselves up to receive God's wavelengths of love and creatively reverberate them out to the world around them. This chapter will explore four case studies that demonstrate conspiring prayer for issues such as racism, accident victims, gun violence, and mental illness.

God always loves to his greatest ability in every moment, respecting our free will and other agencies in the process. This is the amazing truth that fuels my venture into this study of petitionary prayer, and it is something I have come to believe wholeheartedly. The phrase "God is good all the time, and all the time God is good" is not just something that should stir up the congregation on Sunday mornings. It is a truth that can affect every aspect of our theology and practice. God's goodness should also affect our understanding of, and engagement in, petitionary prayer.

We are all preachers and teachers echoing messages we have heard in the past. We can echo the oppressive messages of the surrounding culture. We can echo the painful and belittling messages we received from our family of origin. We can echo the hypervigilant, dark, distrustful, and dehumanizing messages from previous trauma. Or we can listen and echo God's life-giving message of hope, healing, equality, justice, and beauty to those we encounter on our journey. Join me as we come to understand the sacred practice of petitionary prayer more deeply so that the amazing love, beauty, and shalom of God can be wonderfully revealed in a greater measure to the church and to the world.

PART 1
INVESTIGATION

CHAPTER 1

MY JOURNEY INTO PETITIONARY PRAYER

Many years ago, I read Lee Strobel's *The Case for Christ: A Journalist's Personal Investigation of the Evidence for Jesus.* An avowed atheist, Strobel was the legal editor of the *Chicago Tribune* when he set out to investigate the truth claims of Christians. He combed through the evidence, interviewing leading scholars and authorities on the Christian faith. By the end of his journey, instead of debunking Christian beliefs, Strobel had become a committed Christian. In Strobel's introduction to his book, he asks readers to place themselves in the mindset of a juror:

> If you were selected for a jury in a real trial, you would be asked to affirm up front that you haven't formed any pre-conceptions about the case. You would be required to vow that you would be openminded and fair, drawing your conclusions based on the weight of the facts and not on your whims or prejudices. You would be urged to thought-fully consider the credibility of the witnesses, carefully sift the testimony, and rigorously subject the evidence to your common sense and logic.[1]

Thinking of this passage, I wondered what might happen if I applied Strobel's investigative sensibilities and juror mindset to my investigation of petitionary prayer. I decided to take the challenge. While I don't think anyone can be completely unbiased and without preconceived notions, I did try to place my own preconceptions to one side. My goal was to be fair and open-minded. I wanted to base my opinions not only on the truth of Scripture but also on experience, reason, science, and common sense.

I also took my tough questions to the most respected authors, teachers, and pastors I knew of who specialized in the topic of prayer. I didn't want to be a rogue deconstructive agent who was an island unto himself. I knew I needed to wrestle with this issue in community.

While I knew that praying for oneself and for others in close community could be liberating, I began to question the validity of petitionary prayer for others who were not present, as well as for social issues, like poverty, racism, drug addiction, and violence. Does sitting alone in your room praying for God to heal your mom from cancer actually have any effect on her health? Does it have any effect on God and what he chooses to do about her health? Does praying, "God, stop the gun violence in America," increase God's loving capacity to stop violence from occurring? In order to know whether petitionary prayer truly has validity, I needed the courage to ask tough questions like these ones.

FEAR OF REJECTION

According to the latest neuroscience, we all have an innate need to belong, feel safe, and be loved.[2] Our nervous system encodes loneliness, isolation, and rejection as primal threats. Loneliness and isolation can send anxiety and stress hormones rippling through our brains and bodies with devastating consequences to our immune system and overall well-being.[3] Social rejection registers in the same part of the brain as physical pain.[4] Christians tend to fear rejection and isolation from two major figures: God and the church. For many people, it is not easy to separate the two.

For some, the fear of losing God's love, even momentarily, is terrifying. Mother Teresa expressed fear of being rejected by God because of the incessant anxiety and doubt she harbored. She confessed, "So many unanswered questions live within me...I am afraid to uncover them...because of the blasphemy...If there be a God...please forgive me."[5]

Martin Luther, reflecting on his early religious experiences, wrote that he "feared hell somewhat; death, more; failure to please God the judge who made drastic demands, most: 'I trembled.'"[6]

Fearing that the ultimate source of love will vanish and, paradoxically, that the ultimate source of punishment will be left in its wake can be the cause of intense emotional and mental pain. Some people, such as Martin Luther, eventually find a measure of freedom. Unfortunately, many others do not.

Numerous contemporary figures have written of how they were reluctant to share their doubts and questions because they feared being rejected and ostracized by their community. For example, Rachel Held Evans, author of *Searching for Sunday: Loving, Leaving, and Finding the Church,* writes about her Christian community at large:

> My friends and professors diagnosed the crisis of faith as a deliberate act of rebellion. After graduation, rumors of my purported apostasy circulated around town, and I found myself on the prayer request lists of churches I didn't even attend. My best friend wrote me a letter comparing my doubts to a drug habit and explained that she needed to distance herself from me for a while.[7]

Rachel found enough courage to leave her community and turned her experience into something positive. She wrote a book about losing her faith and finding it again. But some cannot find enough strength to leave, and some do not have the courage to stay and share the depths of their struggle with a trusted other. Perhaps at one point they attempted to muster up enough strength to reveal what they truly felt and believed. They took a risk in sharing, and it backfired. All they got was a snide look and a guilt-producing comment. Their panic over the potential loss of love and relationship caused them to ricochet back into the status quo. They were shamed back into regressive conformity and felt forced to hold to homogenous doctrines and values.

Many Christian identities are bound up tightly in their churches. Church is all they know. They grew up in it. Their friends are there. Their families have attended since they were young. The strength it takes to leave and risk the unknown is too great. Because their identities are so closely tied to the community, they have unknowingly allowed themselves to become carbon copies of others instead of the unique individuals God desires them to be. Doubts and questions remain but are locked away deep in the dungeons of their minds, which they fervently hope are escape-proof enough to prevent some ferocious jail break.

As I have wrestled through the topic of petitionary prayer for others, I have felt both excitement and anxiety over the prospect of new theological adventures. Theology, or as one of my former professors defined it, "human talk about human talk about God,"[8] is always morphing and evolving precisely because the people who construct it change. What Christians considered holy at one point in time has been regarded as heretical in another.

For example, at one time many Christians believed the "Curse of Ham" (Genesis 9:20–27) justified racism and slavery. In the past, and even, on occasion, in the present day, Christians have used such verses as "For the husband is the head of the wife as Christ is the head of the church" (Ephesians 5:23) to marginalize women and manipulate them to tolerate abuse and oppression.

In my own exploration of petitionary prayer, my desire has been to swing the theological pendulum toward new emphases and a new trajectory in our praying for others. But though filled with anticipation of what could unfold, I've also felt the anxiety of potential rejection. A part of me knows well that "there is no fear in love, but perfect love drives out fear" (1 John 4:18). But another part has felt afraid that God might not be pleased with my doubts and difficult questions. So I've shoved them down into the recesses of my psyche. But that hasn't always worked.

Sometimes the doubts have lurked in the background like a low-level negative frequency, zapping the zest out of my day. Other times, when I was silent enough, my doubts and questions were joined by condemnation and judgment. Eventually, I came to realize that the nagging, condemning voice coming from the negative frequency was not that of God. Rather, it was a lingering, internalized authoritarian Other with a wagging, critical finger. Some call this a superego. In my case, I think it was past residue from deeply entrenched memories of growing up with a harsh and critical dad—a father whom I desperately tried to please, but to whose standards I could never measure up.

Not only did I have to work through my rejection and abandonment issues with God, I also had to deal with them from my faith community. I knew plenty of Christians who, within their various denominations, would have no problem with questioning the efficacy of certain types of prayer. They might have their unique communal hoops to jump through, but raising questions about whether or not petitionary prayer is effective is not something that would draw harsh condemnation. My own denominational "tribe" was more conservative than many others and not always open to new ideas. I had seen the judgmental way some Christians were treated for questioning what their peers deemed universal truths and sacred.

So I too feared judgment and criticism. I feared losing friends, speaking engagements, and other opportunities, all because I was starting to question the validity of petitionary prayer for others from a distance. We are created to belong. If the tribe where I felt I belonged no longer wanted me, then the prospect of being alone and having to find another tribe felt scary.

Some of those fears proved unfounded. I had imagined the worst possible outcomes, projected them into the minds of other people, and acted as if they were those people's real thoughts toward me. In essence, I'd written a bad script for characters who didn't even know they were in the play.

Unfortunately, once I began my reflective journey, I also found that some of my fears had a genuine basis in reality, and, indeed, I came to face rejection, criticism, and judgment along the way. Some told me I was hell-bound for questioning the inspiration of God's Word. Others deemed me a heretic. Some simply distanced themselves from me. One award-winning Christian editor who started editing my manuscript chose to abandon it midway. She claimed this work would undermine people's faith in the trustworthiness of the Bible. I was semi-shocked and deeply saddened by the way people treated me.

I finally arrived at the place where I simply chose to live life authentically. I wanted to follow my heart as I knew it was in God's loving hands. I preferred suffering the social consequences of exclusion to pretending and living a lie according to other people's religious projections of how I should live and what I should believe. The embodied thought that God loves me as I am and not as others think I should be allowed me to take a theological risk. Therefore, I pressed on.

But before I tell you about where this path took me, let me clarify what I was thinking about and what in particular I had begun to doubt. If you are going to sit with me in a juror seat, you should know who the defendant is. I turn here to a discussion of what exactly prayer is, and specifically what petitionary prayer involves, before returning to the issue of doubt and the need to ask questions in order to pave the way for new theological pathways.

WHAT IS PRAYER?

Prayer is an ancient and sacred practice that has existed as long as humankind has been around. Prayers and sacrifices offered to appease angry gods can be found depicted in cave drawings from the dawn of humanity. Philip and Carol Zaleski, renowned scholars and writers on the topic of religion, write, "Wherever one finds humans, one finds humans at prayer."[9] Some doctors and neuroscientists claim we are literally "wired for God" and have God-sensitive areas in our brains.[10] Therefore, prayer is as natural as drinking or eating. Prayer is such an innate practice that those who claim not to believe in God have been known to call out to him in severe distress (this is sometimes called a "foxhole confession").

Prayer is acknowledgment of, and communication with, a Holy Other. Old Testament scholar Walter Brueggemann defines prayer as follows:

> Prayer is a common, ubiquitous, recurring human prac-
> tice. It is the human reach toward Holy Mystery and Holy
> Ultimacy, an acknowledgment that human persons and

human community are penultimate and stand in response to One who is scarcely accessible but who, in any case, will be addressed.[11]

Prayer is communicating with the Creator of the universe. For some, prayers, by their very nature, demonstrate a hierarchy in which one is subservient and submissive and the Other is holy and transcendent. For others, prayer is primarily based on a deep friendship with God and a valuing of his immanence and closeness. For most people, prayers are an attempt to reach out, or inward, to connect and communicate with the mysterious known/unknown God.

Prayers are not magical incantations or secret coded messages wrapped in sacred energy. To pray simply means *to talk to God*. Try this thought experiment. Let's assume you have been praying for your ailing mom. Repeat this sentence out loud: "I have been *praying* that God heals my mom." Now say, "I have been *talking to* God about healing my mom." You may experience a subtle shift between the two and a slight awkwardness or discomfort. Simply substituting the word "praying" with "talking" has the potential to reduce the type of thinking that views prayer as a magical incantation or another form of superstition while increasing its relational component.

There are dozens of ways to pray to God. You can pray prayers of consecration, exaltation, lament, and petition. You can pray joyful prayers of thanksgiving or angry prayers of protest. Your prayers can be bullets—very focused and precise—or buckshot—praying tangentially on any topic that comes to mind. You can pray in the wilderness, in the bathroom, on the beach, at work, or anywhere you want because God is everywhere.

Prayer can also be expanded to include pouring out one's talent, time, energy, and resources to the glory of God. Glynn

Cardy, the vicar at The Community of Saint Luke in New Zealand writes:

> Prayer is more than thoughts or words directed at or toward a deity. It is more, too, than silent contemplation. It is, rather, a way of embodying a vision that encompasses thoughts, words, and silence, as well as sipping coffee, laughing, being arrested, and making love. Prayer then is a big word, which describes how to live out faith. St. Paul's admonition to "pray without ceasing" (1 Thess. 5:17) only makes sense if it means to live one's faith.[12]

Jesus is a prime example of someone who lived his life as an unceasing prayer to God. Not only was he praying on the many occasions when he rose well before dawn to speak to God, but his entire life was a prayer and a sweet aroma unto God. When Jesus held precious children, fought for lepers and healed them, reached out to those considered sinners, losers, or lunatics, or spoke against the religious leaders of his day, he was the full embodiment of a prayerful life.

PETITIONARY PRAYER

Petitionary prayer is a specific form of prayer aimed at making requests of God. Christian philosophers and theologians Bruce Benson and Norman Wirzba define petitionary prayer as follows:

> Whatever other things [petitionary] prayer does, at bottom, and what distinguishes it from praise and confession, with which it no doubt bears close relations, structurally and in practice, is that prayer is the sending of a request or question to the Other and thus the seeking of an answer, the asking of the Other to respond to me, to be responsible.[13]

Petitionary prayers make requests of God for answers to life's questions and concerns. They are also pleas for God to be the sole responsible agent to act on behalf of the one who is praying. Petitionary prayers can be offered on a small and personal scale for oneself or for others, or they may involve requests on a larger scale that concern changing undesirable circumstances within society or, indeed, the world as a whole.

While there are petitionary prayers that ask God to continue the wonderful work that he is already doing, I define the traditional understanding of the typical petitionary prayer as *talking to God and asking God to love in a specific manner in which God was not doing so beforehand.*

For example, if I prayed, "God, please save my uncle Harold from his drug addiction," I would be assuming that before I started praying, God was not already actively loving in the specific manner requested. In other words, God was not saving my uncle Harold from his drug addiction. I would be offering my petition in the hope that God might hear my prayer and lovingly save my uncle. If I believed God was currently saving my uncle Harold from his drug addiction, I would pray prayers of thanksgiving and not prayers of petition. Petitionary prayer of this kind, especially as it is practiced by Christians who pray for others from a distance in the hope that God will bring healing or some other change, is what we are calling to question in this book.

DOUBTING PRAYER

Deconstructing the sacred practice of petitionary prayer on behalf of others is no easy task. It has been performed for thousands of years across all theistic religions and is a staple in churches across the world. The last thing I desire is to be deemed a heretic and ostracized by the Christian community. Anyone who has ever questioned the status quo regarding any revered Christian doctrine or practice knows the anxiety it provokes.

Still, a part of me was not able to shake a nagging fear that petitionary prayers for sick or hurting people from a distance, or for systemic injustice or world catastrophes, could very well be like rubbing a rabbit's foot for good luck. It might help the person rubbing the rabbit's foot feel better, but that is all that occurs. At least that was one of my fears as I began this investigative journey.

It seems that I am not alone in wondering about petitionary prayer. The issue of whether prayer makes a difference in the lives of Christians is an ancient question. For example, a concerned spiritual seeker sought wisdom from the early church father Origen (233 CE) about the conundrum of petitionary prayer:

> First, if God foreknows what will come to be and if it must happen, then prayer is in vain. Second, if everything happens according to God's will and if what he wills is fixed and no one of the things He wills can be changed, then prayer is in vain.[14]

I have also found myself in non-heretical good company with the well-respected C. S. Lewis. He penned an essay entitled "Petitionary Prayer: A Problem Without an Answer" in which he wrote:

> The problem I am submitting to you arises not about prayer in general but only about that kind of prayer which consists of request or petition…. I have no answer to my problem, though I have taken it to about every Christian I know.[15]

That is not to say Lewis never found satisfying answers to his questions. But I feel comforted knowing he had the guts to ask them in the first place.

Having doubts and questions about something is what provides the raw material for innovation and creativity. In this case, having doubts and questions about petitionary prayer has the potential to call forth new prayer-filled pathways to shalom. Without doubts and questions, we would be stuck in the Stone Age. Doubting and questioning are, in part, what enables positive changes in society and across history, such as the abolishment of slavery, the empowerment of women to vote, the research undertaken to save lives with vaccines, the technology used to create computers and to take us to the moon, the raising of the minimum wage, and the crafting of new genres of music to name but a few instances. Can doubts and questions assist petitionary prayer in becoming more liberating and valuable? I hoped so.

Sybil MacBeth, author of *Praying in Color: Drawing a New Path to God*, started asking questions concerning prayer. She questioned whether Christians were too narrow in their understanding of prayer and wondered if there was an alternative approach for those who did not prefer praying in words. She developed a creative approach to prayer that uses colors, doodling, circles, shapes, and drawings as a primary method of connecting with God. MacBeth writes:

> Adopting a new way of praying may require a *suspension of rigid belief*.... Holding and worshiping the stone tablet of my 'I've always done it this way' prayers is idolatry.[16]

Nothing should be off limits to doubts, questions, and curiosity, including prayer. But while doubting and questioning can be beneficial, how we go about these issues is important. Evangelical author, speaker, and pastor John Ortberg writes, "Doubt is a good servant but a poor master."[17] In other words, the key to doubting is to doubt well. Expressing our doubts with a few other people who are safe, trustworthy, and loving, along with the Spirit of Truth, is the perfect way to doubt. Too much analysis alone is a prescription for paralysis. Conversing with people we trust helps us to feel loved and becomes a life-giving sustenance to get through any difficult terrain that lies ahead.

The quest to live out an earthly faith that makes a heavenly difference was a huge catalyst in my journey regarding prayer. Living in a real world with real people and real horrors that seem to multiply on a daily basis demands that we live out a vibrant and practical faith, which also means that praying the right kinds of prayers matters. If traditional petitionary prayer for others is not the most transformative prayer to pray, or, at worst, is a superstitious practice, we need to rethink it. We should prioritize the reimagination of petitionary prayer because it may make a greater impact *for* those we love and *upon* the rampant injustice we see in the world.

To determine whether traditional petitionary prayer is the best option to increase God's loving activity in the world, we must examine closely just what such prayer involves. We must ask tough questions about the "mechanics" of prayer; that is, we must ask how prayer works and how effective it is in accomplishing the goal it seeks to achieve. It is to a discussion of these matters that I now turn in chapter two.

CHAPTER 2

WHAT ARE THE MECHANICS OF PETITIONARY PRAYER?

I know the Bible tells us to pray petitionary prayers. For many, that makes it a done deal. "The Bible says it, so I believe it, and I will obey it," they declare proudly.

There are many days when I envy that simple faith. Unfortunately, that kind of faith is not so easy for me. I am like a curious kid who, after being firmly told by his parents to do something, asks why and then wants to hear more than just, "Because we are your parents, and we said so."

Yes, the Bible says to do it. And yet, I can't help but be perplexed by the practice of petitionary prayer. I want to know why, and, more specifically, how prayer works. I've asked fellow pastors and scholars this very question, and here are a few of the answers I received:

- Prayer is powerful, and it affects God and the outcome.

- Prayer works because of the butterfly effect.

- Prayer is spiritual warfare, activating and releasing God's supernatural power.

- Prayer increases the probability of love and healing as God weaves those effects into the tapestry of His divine purpose.

One pastor tried to encourage me by giving me a quote from E. M. Bounds, an author who is well-known for his many books on the topic of prayer:

> The concentration and aggregation of faith, desire, and prayer increased the volume of spiritual force until it became overwhelming and irresistible in its power. Units of prayer combined, like droplets of water, make an ocean which defies resistance.[1]

What in the world is Bounds talking about? What is the "volume of spiritual force"? What does he mean by "power"? What are "units of prayer"? Do they have something to do with mathematics? What does he mean by "an ocean which defies resistance"? I get that his phrasing here is poetic, but is there real substance behind it? Is it all inspiring fluff, or do the words have a direct correlation to reality?

The majority of responses to my follow-up questions from these pastors and scholars could be summarized this way: "Mark, have faith. It works. The Bible commands us to do it, so just do it. Please, no more questions." Anytime I hear someone become annoyed and say, "No more questions," I begin to wonder if that phrase is code for, "I am getting anxious because your questions are causing me to question my own faith. Your questions are exposing my own lack of understanding of prayer. So, cut it out and stop asking provocative questions."

Hearing such ambiguous responses simply piqued my curiosity even further. I put on my metaphorical scuba gear, dove deep down, invited the Spirit to join me, and began asking myself such questions as:

- I know prayer is a deeply relational practice, but what are the mechanics behind this profound practice called prayer?

- What exactly happens after the words leave my lips or after I speak them silently? Does God instantly hear them, or do they first move through the traffic of heaven where angels and demons are engaged in an epic battle?

- Some have suggested prayer releases and activates God's power. Are prayers, then, like magical incantations?

- When a person prays for God to heal their ill dad, does that give God extra power, energy, or motivation to do so?

- Is God busy doing something else, so that prayers are a necessary reminder for God to heal that person's dad?

- Is persistent petitionary prayer performed simply to annoy God, so that God will eventually, although begrudgingly, do the right thing and answer those prayers, as in the parable of the persistent widow and uncaring judge (Luke 18:1–8)?

- If petitionary prayers are so effective, why does so much evil still occur in places where there are faithful and praying churches?

- Is more prayer better? Does God increase his active love because a larger number of people pray? Does God say, "Well, just twenty of you prayed. If thirty of you had prayed, I would definitely have healed him"?

- What specifically does someone praying that God heal their dad do *to* or *for* God that would increase God's active love in that dad's life? Does God *unilaterally intervene* when enough people pray? If a virus, for instance, is attacking the dad's cells, will God personally go inside those cells and destroy the virus without cooperation from other agencies, such as medical personnel and/or the body's own immune system?

- If praying to God moves him to action, would he refuse to act and allow people to suffer or even die because people did not pray? If the ailing dad did not have any prayers offered to God on his behalf, would God simply allow him to die because of this?

- If some prayers seem to get answered while others of a similar nature do not, does this mean God chooses which prayers to answer? Does he choose to ignore some because they go against his desires?

- If an all-powerful God could single-handedly save and deliver loved ones but allows them to get into fatal accidents, become sick, get raped, or experience other tragedies because people did not pray for them, is that consistent with what a loving God would do?

The more I asked Christians about my nagging questions, the more I realized too many Christians don't have a clue how prayer works. The cat was out of the bag. Something was amiss. I could no longer settle for the tip-of-the-tongue memorized clichés. My cognitive dissonance was screaming for resolution to this petitionary puzzle.

I was not necessarily looking for a scientific explanation, but I was looking for a logical and coherent one, something other than, "It just works." My theology of petitionary prayer also had to dance well with my theodicy. Praying to a God who automatically and single-handedly changes the outcome of situations and the people in them would be different than praying to a

God who cannot coerce or control but requires cooperation to achieve loving outcomes. Petitionary prayer also had to make sense from what we know of science and our lived experience. Unfortunately, the more I inquired about the nuances of how petitionary prayer worked, the more concerned I became.

THE BIBLE AND THE
MECHANICS OF PRAYER

Some have told me, "Mark, there are biblical texts which clearly encourage petitionary prayer for others." I agree. There are numerous places where people pray, petition, and have their prayers answered (e.g., Luke 1:13; Romans 10:1; Ephesians 6:18; Philippians 1:19; 4:6; 1 Timothy 2:1). We will explore some of the most important passages that touch on petitionary prayer in chapter five, although we will only be able to scratch the surface. A comprehensive review of all the pertinent biblical texts related to petitionary prayer would span many volumes.

Until we get there, it is important to remember that while biblical writers and saints of old believed petitionary prayer for others was powerful and brought about miraculous events, they were culturally conditioned. Their understanding was limited to the amount of revelation they could comprehend at their time in history. It is possible they did not think through the nuances, mechanics, and implications of petitionary prayer. They did not consider how other agencies were involved in moment-to-moment events—agencies like free will, lawlike regularities, randomness, and God's uncontrolling, loving character.[2] They engaged in an ancient social and sacred practice that came naturally and was modeled by generations of spiritual seekers before them.

Paul asks the Ephesians to "pray also for me, that whenever I speak, words may be given to me so that I will fearlessly make known the mystery of the gospel, for which I am an ambassador in chains. Pray that I may declare it fearlessly, as I should" (Ephesians 6:19–20). There is no doubt that Paul encourages petitionary prayer for himself and others. To give a modern comparison, Paul's prayer echoes the types of request I see all the time on Facebook:

- "Pray for me. I am preaching a sermon tomorrow. I want God to speak through me in wisdom and power."

- "I am taking a test tomorrow. Pray that I do well."

- "Pray for me to remember my lines for my audition."

Paul and others may have had a vague sense that something better may occur because of prayer, but, ultimately, I don't think they thought through the nuances of their requests. My sense is that some of Paul's prayers, as well as those of others, are ultimately community-forming acts; the people making the requests feel comforted knowing others are praying for them. Paul asking the Ephesians to pray for him is code for, "I want to embrace God's boldness and preach a powerful message for the glory of God, but I am a little fearful. Stand with me in solidarity." Asking for prayer is another way to feel that you are not alone in your difficult circumstances.

While Paul wrote about the power of prayer, he did not address the mechanics of prayer in any of his writings. Given this, I propose that Paul may not have asked profound theological and philosophical questions regarding prayer. The same can be said of many Christians today. Most of the people I ask about how prayer works simply have no clue. I don't say this to shame or belittle them. Heck, I didn't start thinking about the nuances of prayer until twenty-two years after becoming a Christian. Even now, I have only begun to dip my toe into the deep waters surrounding the mysteries of prayer.

We all experience traditions passed down to us that we seldom question. For example, one day, I realized that I asked people, "How are you doing?" without having the time, or sometimes the interest, to actually care how they were doing. It was an unconscious social norm that felt right in the moment, but one that I had never previously questioned. After realizing what I did, I began to reflect on the practice and come up with another greeting that felt more appropriate. Following such conventions comes to us naturally as we learn our behavior and, in turn, it is positively reinforced by others around us who are all following and responding to these same conventions. Unthinkingly greeting someone in this way may be similar to what is going on with those who unthinkingly ask for prayer in the Bible, maybe even to Paul.

When Paul asked for prayer, did he imagine God withholding boldness until others asked God to give it to him? Did Paul reflect on the character of God and question why a good and loving God would withhold it in the first place? Did Paul think that the more people prayed for him, the greater the chance of the prayers tipping God's scale? That after a certain amount of prayer, God would grant the request? Did Paul question why God wouldn't give boldness in response to his individual prayer apart from the prayers of the Ephesians? Did Paul wonder about God's will? In other words, if it was God's will to give Paul boldness, how could anything, including lack of prayer, stop God from pouring out boldness? Did Paul think that God, because of the saints' prayers, would instantly upload boldness to him through his Spirit?

I am doubtful that Paul asked these kinds of questions. Paul wrestled with the relevant issues of his time; the conundrum of prayer and its mechanics was not one of them. Though Paul was brilliant, for him, prayer seemed simple: We pray, and we request prayer, we believe it is important and powerful, and we trust God will answer the prayer if it is in accordance with his will. That attitude is the same for many Christians today. For most, prayer is a practice of the heart rather than of the brain; it is not something analyzed and thought through like a complex math equation.

A DEVELOPING VIEW OF PRAYER

Prayer is as ancient a practice as they come. Is it possible that there are some superstitious elements in the practice that we could let go of? Is it possible that petitionary prayer could receive a makeover, especially keeping in mind the texts of the Bible, science, experience, and the uncontrolling, loving character of God?

The Trinity is an example of a doctrine that has developed over time. The biblical writers grew in their understanding of the Trinity, a growth that is especially evident as you consider the progression from the Hebrew Bible saints to the New Testament saints. As a matter of fact, the doctrine of the Trinity was not conceptualized in its current form until about the fourth century, and since then it has expanded in scope and nuance.

The Trinity as understood by modern believers would have been quite foreign to most of the biblical writers. The writers of the New Testament had a simplistic notion of the existence of the Father, Son, and Holy Spirit. Matthew records Jesus's words, "Go and make disciples of all nations, baptizing them in the name of the Father and of the Son and of the Holy Spirit"

(Matthew 28:19). If you had asked Matthew whether the Father, Son, and Holy Spirit exist, he would have said, "Of course!" But if you had asked for details about how they worked together, what their essence was, and what their unique roles were in creation, salvation, and sanctification, he may have not been as articulate as some are today.

I suggest that the same dynamic of progressive revelation that occurred with the Trinity is now occurring with our understanding of prayer. The term "progressive" is not meant to suggest "better-than." It is used in the sense of *building upon* and *complementing.* Any knowledge obtained today is built upon the incredible wisdom and revelation that has come before us.

In the next chapters, I hope to advance that progress by exploring some of the nuances and mechanics of prayer that Paul and the other authors of the New Testament did not specifically address in Scripture. We will begin by exploring the critical theological and philosophical problems with petitionary prayer as it is traditionally understood.

PART 2

DECONSTRUCTION

CHAPTER 3

UNFORESEEN THEOLOGICAL AND PHILOSOPHICAL PITFALLS OF PETITIONARY PRAYER

One cool Autumn evening, Debby Connors spit the toothpaste into the sink, set her toothbrush in the charger, and dried her hands. She was cringing thinking about the last conversation she had about God with her college-aged son, Jason. Since his sophomore year of high school, he seemed to be rejecting even the idea of God more and more. Coming back into her bedroom, her bed looked awfully inviting after a long day of work at the hospital. Her knees popped as she knelt beside her bed; she wasn't as young as she used to be. After going through her usual thanksgivings to God, she anxiously lifted Jason up in prayer, as she did every night. "God pour out your love on Jason. Please save him."

Well-meaning Christians like Debby pray similar prayers for their unsaved loved ones every day throughout the world. What these Christians don't realize, however, is the underlying implications of these prayers for one's perception of God.

If you were to ask Debby whether she believes that God is unaware of Jason's need to be saved, her offended reply would probably come back as, "Most certainly not!". The conversation could continue as you ask Debby whether she believes that God does not want Jason to be saved. "Of course, he does!" Debby would reply. The follow-up question might be to ask whether God should force Jason to do something against his will, which would provoke an inevitable answer of, "He needn't do anything of the sort!" One might follow this with the simple question, "Why, then, are you praying?"

When Debby describes her loving and compassionate God in her answers to these questions, her description is at complete odds with the ignorant, ill-willed and manipulative God that is implied by Debby's prayer—a prayer that has to beg to receive God's help to save Debby's beloved son. The focus of this chapter is to examine petitionary prayer on behalf of others. Scripture certainly encourages petitionary prayers *for* oneself and others. Such prayers are indisputably rewarding, as demonstrated by both research and anecdotal evidence. But while petitionary prayer *on behalf* of others is, without question, biblical and potentially effectual, the topic also raises both critical concerns and important practical and theological questions.

While petitionary prayer for others can be carried out in a theologically mature manner, the practice has potential pitfalls. In offering such petitions, we may be unintentionally questioning the wisdom and goodness of God while failing to take human free will into account. Depending on our view of God, we might also be unknowingly portraying God as an intentionally passive bystander to evil, as well as someone who shows favoritism.

As you continue reading, you may not be convinced by my assessment regarding traditional petitionary prayer practices. That is okay. I have never met two Christians who think exactly alike on most topics. But at the very least, I hope the following discussion leads you to reflect on prayer in a new way and to further develop and deepen your own theology of prayer—even if it is at odds with the one I propose.

IS GOD ILL-WILLED?

There are a few common conundrums raised by our traditional understandings of petitionary prayer. For example, what is the point of praying if God already knows all about the situation we are praying for? If a boy whose father is a renowned mathematician tells his dad, "Dad, two plus two equals four," he does not inform his dad of anything new. Likewise, when a little girl prays, "God, my dad is sick. Could you heal him?" she is not informing God of something he did not already know.

And since God already knows about the situation we are praying for, God doesn't need us to pray wordy prayers, as Jesus himself made clear in his Sermon on the Mount (Matthew 6:7–8). So the question becomes, "If God knows about our need before we ask, why ask God at all?" Though this common concern and others like it are interesting questions to pursue, they have plausible explanations.[1] We want to explore different territory.

One of the biggest conundrums with petitionary prayers for others is that they can unknowingly suggest a diminished view of God's loving nature. In petitionary prayer, we are asking God to do *our will* with respect to our loved ones. We ask God to keep them safe, to heal them, to give them success, or to save them from an eternity without him. We want these things for those close to us because we love them. But if God loves them too, and his love far exceeds our love, does he not want these things for them too?

Embedded in some petitionary prayers is an assumption that God is not already performing or seeking to perform the requested action. Praying for God to love, heal, and be gracious to loved ones suggests that God is not loving, healing, and being gracious to them. It's like asking a world-renowned heart surgeon, known for her skill and compassion, who is in the middle of performing heart surgery on your spouse, "Can you perform the surgery with skill, professionalism, wisdom, and care?" Many petitionary prayers question God's goodness without the petitioner realizing it.

Another manner in which petitionary prayer can portray a less-than-loving God is by painting a picture of a God who is being stingy with his love and who will only release his love if we beg him. The image being projected is that the more we cajole God with prayer, the more likely God will be to cease being passive, get off his throne, and engage in the loving action desired. This is the unspoken logic behind prayer chains. Prayer chains assume that the more people are praying to God, the more likely God is to answer the request. They imply that God can singlehandedly carry out the request and reduce suffering after one prayer, but God chooses to wait for a certain number of people to make the request to intervene. Let's examine some of the above conundrums and inadequate portrayals of God in the situation involving Debby praying for her son, Jason.

Debby prays petitionary prayers daily for her unsaved son. She believes that prayer works. She is convinced that the more she prays, the more likely it will be that God will act on her behalf. She desperately hopes her devout prayers will cause God to intervene and save her son.

"God, pour out your love on Jason," she prays daily. "Please save him." While her motive of concern about the well-being of her child is pure, she is unknowingly praying prayers that are not in alignment with the reality of the profound goodness of God. Scott Davison, professor of philosophy at Morehead State University, wrestles with whether petitionary prayer may sometimes suggest a lack of trust in God when he writes:

> If I were to ask God to do something specific for my children that I could not do myself, that could suggest a lack of trust in God to look after my children. It could suggest that I was worried that God would not realize the importance of this issue or would not help my children unless I asked—even though (according to traditional theism) God loves them even more than I do and knows more than I do what they need.[2]

Debby prays for God to be a loving God ("pour out your love on Jason"), which is inherently problematic for one overwhelming reason: God has always loved Jason and is presently loving Jason, even while his mother is praying. God is also seeking to save Jason—mind, body, and spirit. A person does not need to twist God's arm or talk him into doing what automatically flows out of God's nature and character. Is God good some of the time or all of the time?

God is always loving (1 John 4:16, 19; Ephesians 3:16–19) and always seeking to save (Luke 19:10; Titus 2:11; 1 Timothy 2:4). God is actively good all the time, not just when we pray for him to be good. Although Debby prays to God because she believes God is good, her very prayer unwittingly questions God's goodness.

Let me use another story as illustration. A man named Sam recommends his friend's renowned Michelin-starred restaurant to a relative. His friend is known to be one of the most competent, hardworking, and passionate chefs in the business. Upon hearing that the relative made a reservation, Sam decides to call his Michelin-starred chef friend.

How do you think Sam's friend would feel if Sam asked him to make sure he washed his hands before cooking and to kindly prepare a delicious meal for his relative when he came in? Such a request would imply doubt in his friend's competence and ignore his stellar reputation, skill, and expertise. It would mean that Sam has a distorted image of his friend. If he really knew his friend and trusted him, he would not have had to ask for what was already a given.

A Christian who prays, "God, please don't hate me," is praying a theologically incorrect prayer because a God of love cannot hate us (John 3:16). Such a prayer doubts the goodness of God. A struggling Christian who fears God's punishment and prays, "God, please don't pour out your wrath on me," also prays a prayer that is contrary to God's loving nature (1 Thessalonians 5:9). The same can be said of a Christian who prays, "God, grant my dad traveling mercies," as though God must be petitioned to protect his children from danger. The implication of such a prayer is that God may allow any Christian who doesn't pray for traveling mercies to be harmed on the road due to lack of prayer. Likewise, a Christian who prays, "God, pour out your love and save my son," as though God is withholding his love from her son and intentionally choosing not to save him, is praying in a manner that is theologically contradictory to God's loving nature and perfect will.

PRIORITIZING POWER AND NEGLECTING FREE WILL

The problem with the above petitions is that they primarily keep God's *autocratic* power in mind. Take the mother praying for her son's salvation. Her prayer conveys that God is an autocrat. That is, God is in utmost control, has absolute power, and, if he just chose to do so, could single-handedly save her son with complete disregard for the son's free will and agency. This mother believes that an extra dose of God's mercy is what is keeping her son from being saved. She hopes God will hear her through her faithfulness and fervent prayer, change his mind, and save her son.

Alternatively, we could keep in mind God's *loving* power. God's power is always demonstrated through the prism of his love. Thomas Jay Oord reminds us that love doesn't unilaterally control, force, or compel others.[3] Similarly, referring to God's inspiration (or "breathing," 2 Timothy 3:16) in the lives of the biblical writers and in our own, American theologian Gregory Boyd writes:

> God refuses to undermine the personhood and freedom of people by lobotomizing them so that they perfectly conform to his will.... God respects the integrity of a mutually impacting relationship, which is what a relationship of love requires.[4]

Theologian Paul Fiddes writes:

> We often project a worldly idea of power on to God. We attribute to God political notions of power, assuming that it means coerciveness, being able to compel others to do what we want.[5]

Autocratic power in a chaotic world can soothe our anxieties, but to think of God in such a way distorts our perception of his loving and uncontrolling nature, which in turn affects the way we pray. If our image of God is that of an autocrat, we believe God can do whatever God wants whenever God wants and however God wants to do it. Therefore, we don't consider human agency and free will in the prayer equation. When we hold to such an autocratic image of God, we can become like hungry dogs beneath the master's table waiting for delicious scraps to fall. We plead and beg for the crumbs of God's love to fall from heaven because he is the one with all of the power to heal, save, and deliver loved ones.

The problem with such an autocratic image of God is that God is not the only one with power, control, and responsibility. *People* have plenty of (God-given) power, control, and responsibility, too. As we will discuss in chapter six, since we are not robots and God's nature is love, there are some things that God cannot do. God does not override our free will, therefore he cannot single-handedly control people. Instead, he lovingly draws people to himself and waits patiently for us to embrace his graceful invitations. C. Robert Mesle, a professor of philosophy and religion at Graceland University in Lamoni, Iowa, writes:

> Every creature in the universe is continually experiencing the divine love. This love is the very foundation of freedom and of love within all creatures. This gracious—unmerited—love is continually poured into all creation. The choice lies with us how we will respond. We have the power to accept or reject that love and the call it involves.[6]

While there are many who may not consciously experience God's divine, unmerited love, every person and all of creation experience this love in some way, shape, or form. It is because of God's gracious love that he does not want "anyone to perish but everyone to come to repentance" (2 Peter 3:9). God is loving, convicting, and saving to the extent that people open their hearts to receive such grace. God does not force or coerce love. We have the power and agency to accept or reject God's extravagant love.

Let us return to Debby, the mother who prays to God for her son, Jason. Even though God's love came first (1 John 4:19), Jason, through God's gift of faith alongside the synergy of God's love, must have a "come to Jesus" moment (most likely one of thousands he will have in his lifetime). Jason's heart has a door with a lock on the inside. The Spirit gives him the key, and they unlock it together. When it is unlocked, Jesus does not barge through. Jesus knocks, but Jason must open the door from the inside (Revelation 3:20).

In the Gospel of Matthew, Jesus not only reveals his merciful love for his people but also offers a window into their true freedom. With what must be a heavy heart, he says, "Jerusalem, Jerusalem … how often I have longed to gather your children together, as a hen gathers her chicks under her wings." Jesus then tells us how the people of Jerusalem responded: "You were not willing" (Matthew 23:37).

Because God is uncontrolling love, he doesn't force relationships. All the petitionary prayers in the world cannot move God to control Jason like a robot and flick a salvation switch. Jason must willingly confess with his mouth, believe in his heart, and accept the grace that has been offered him (Romans 10:9–10).

Countless people die without ever coming to know Jesus even though their parents have faithfully prayed for them their whole lives. Some thinkers make sense of this harsh reality by believing God chose, purposed, and predestined such people to never know Jesus intimately and to spend their eternities in hell and horrific torment (along with billions of other unbelievers from throughout time). Therefore, no matter how many people pray for such a person, they can never be saved because they were not chosen.

Others, like me, believe people must freely accept God's offer of salvation. It cannot be forced on them. Rather than believing God chose some individuals to spend eternity in hell, unable to experience his loving and intimate presence, I believe that God gave people a free choice to accept or reject his grace. Therefore, until someone is willing, petitionary prayers will not do anything to change the outcome.

Am I suggesting we don't pray for our loved ones? Not at all! Prayer can be a wonderful way to share our hearts with God, and God relishes those times when we talk with him. But a mother's petition can neither force nor convince God to unilaterally control her son and force him to follow God. Professor of philosophy Bruce R. Reichenbach writes, "Prayers requesting that God bring particular persons to love and serve him must be prayed with the realization that God wants their free, not coerced, response."[7] If Jason says yes to God, you can rest assured that God is the first to arrive at the scene. God doesn't need prayers to convince him to do so.

GOD MUST BE PASSIVE AND CRUEL

Our traditional concept of petitionary prayer raises another conundrum. If it takes our prayers for God to increase his active and tangible love in the lives of struggling human beings, it is logical to assume that when people do not pray for others, God intentionally withholds his love from those others. God could single-handedly save, heal, and deliver those others, but because no one has prayed for him to do so, he does not. For example, philosopher Isaac Choi writes of petitionary prayer, "God may choose not to maximize the good in people's lives in order to allow for the effects of these (sometimes intercontinental) acts of love between his creatures."[8] In other words, God halts his loving action in the world to allow others to pray. The prayers then affect the outcome by moving God and others to maximize the good in others' lives.

The logic of such an argument is as follows. God could unilaterally increase his active love in the world and maximize the good in certain people's lives. He chooses not to because other people did not make a choice to pray for these people. God, the very definition of love, allows people to become sick, to miss rent payments, to remain unregenerate, and to be raped or murdered just because other people did not pray for them to get well, have rent money, become saved, or stay safe. Such logic distorts God's image into one of passiveness and even cruelty; God becomes a bystander who simply watches people suffer while doing nothing to stop the evil in their lives from occurring, despite having the power to do so.

Philosopher and Christian apologist Paul Copan tries to reconcile the power of prayer and God's sovereignty. Copan's view of petitionary prayer for others exemplifies my concern over such an image of God's passivity amidst human suffering. Copan writes:

> You hear a friend of yours is in an auto accident, but you don't yet know whether he's alive or not. What good will prayer do since he's in fact either alive or dead? Well, God knows how you'll freely pray in response to hearing the news of this accident; so, in his foreknowledge, he may have worked out his purposes in advance so that your friend would live in direct response to the prayer you offered up— but die if you hadn't. The prayer of a righteous person can accomplish much (James 5:16)![9]

Really? If Copan's reader hadn't prayed for this hypothetical, injured friend, the friend would have died? God will intervene if the reader does pray but won't otherwise? God lets people live or die simply because others do or don't talk to him and ask him to intervene on their behalf? Additionally, what were God's "purposes" in this scenario? Did God purposefully orchestrate and intricately design the accident? Did God purpose or compel the reader to pray? I find Copan's view of God, a view shared by many Christians, contradictory to a God whose nature is pre-eminently loving.

Copan's view is also problematic because it does not consider a friend who dies despite being surrounded by prayers for continued life. What would it mean if the injured friend had died and yet had been prayed for? Would the friend's death mean God had willfully chosen to ignore the prayer? If the action to save the friend's life was in the hands of the one offering the prayer to God, whose hands would the death of the friend have fallen into? We cannot say that the friend would not die if he had been prayed for; people die every day in similar circumstances, despite prayer.

There is another problem with this way of thinking. How can we be responsible for praying and making a difference in the lives of others if we can never know for sure whether our prayers make any difference? For example, why would God choose not to save the life of the injured man in the car accident solely because his friend didn't pray for him? For what reason? One could never know for certain whether the lack of prayer allowed the victim to die, so what is the valuable lesson to be learned? God is also not in the habit of saying things like, "Good job! Your talking to me did the trick," when events turn out the way we've prayed.

The reality is that God is always actively loving, with or without our prayers. As finite creatures, we cannot comprehend the incredibly beautiful and intricate ways in which God loves people and creation. He doesn't show favorites (Romans 2:11), and he continually rains love and blessings upon the righteous and unrighteous alike (Matthew 5:45) without needing specific prayers to do so.

If, on the one hand, God routinely intervenes in people's lives without specific prayers for them and, on the other, chooses to remain passive and do nothing simply because people haven't prayed, the logical conclusion is that God is a cruel utilitarian, prioritizing the faith of some over the health of others, rather than a benevolent Father to all. British theologians Peter and Charlotte Vardy rightly ask:

> Why did God not come to Hitler or Stalin, causing them to use their powers for human good rather than evil? The idea that God is so selective is difficult to reconcile with the idea of God as omnibenevolent.[10]

Atheistic philosopher Georges Rey adds his voice to those who are uneasy about a God who allows people to suffer because other people are not praying for them. He writes:

> The idea of an omni-god that would permit, for example, children to die slowly of leukemia is already pretty puzzling; but to permit this to happen unless someone prays to Him to prevent it—this verges on a certain sort of sadism and moral incoherence (imagine a doctor who acted in this way!), and one wonders what people have in mind in worshipping Him.[11]

The idea that God allows children, or anyone for that matter, to suffer and die because people do not pray is just one distortion of our image of God. There are other nuances of beliefs around prayer that distort, or even mangle, our understanding of God's loving nature. For example, Jerome Gellman, a philosophy professor at Ben-Gurion University of the Negev in Beer-Sheva, Israel, suggests that God brings evil on people precisely to spur them on to prayer. He writes:

> Are we to believe God would visit suffering upon a person, let alone an entire people, just for the purpose of having them pray to God? Does this not oppose God's perfect goodness? No, it does not. Granted, it might be immoral for an earthly parent to act this way toward her child. Even so, it is not immoral for God to act in this way toward us.[12]

The idea that God allows evil events to occur because people do not talk to him and intentionally plans evil and harm to cause people to talk to him is in complete contradiction to any normal definition of love; indeed, such behavior could safely be deemed manipulative and abusive. Why would God be exempt from a common-sense notion of morality, considering that any true morality itself flows from God's own nature? As the author suggests, it would be completely immoral for a parent to do such a thing to a child. It would be cruel, and, depending on the act, the parent could be arrested for child abuse. God should be the exemplar of loving acts, not someone who tells us, "Do as I say, not as I do."

Georges Rey and other deep-thinking theologians and philosophers who share his concerns have a valid point. There is a moral incoherence and inherent contradiction in the idea that God requires petitionary prayer before he increases his loving action in the world to stop evil. A God who can intervene and stop evil in its tracks but chooses when and where not to do so is logically and morally incomprehensible. Or, as Oord puts it, "It is hard to believe God loves perfectly if God is capable of total control but fails to prevent genuine evil. God remains culpable."[13]

For thousands of years, religious people across countless cultures may have believed that if they didn't pray and appease their fickle gods, their crops and lives could be ruined. The view was that God would send calamities upon people and withhold blessings because devotees were not continually offering prayers and sacrifices to him. But such belief is not tenable for the Christian, especially if we keep God's uncontrolling and powerful love in mind.

In thinking about petitionary prayer, we can no longer settle for, "Well, it's a mystery." What would we think of a man watching a child being sexually assaulted, who has the power to do something about it but chooses not to because no one asked him? The Spirit of love and justice within us would rise up and object that such a man was unjust and immoral. This same Spirit would also rise up against a view of God as someone with full ability to intervene in horrific events but who simply chooses not to. God has given us a brain and common sense. God has also given us *Jesus sense*. In other words, if the actions and characteristics that we claim to be those of God do not appear to line up with the God we see revealed fully in Christ, we have a right to question the validity and origin of such claims.

MISSIONAL THEOLOGY

A man once came into my therapy office to speak with me about his difficulties concentrating at work. He also struggled with anxiety and suffered from insomnia. After a brief conversation, I asked him if he took any solace in faith or spirituality.

His demeanor changed instantly. His face started to flush, and he raised his voice. "Screw God! God allowed my praying and faithful Christian wife to die in a car accident. I'm left with our three kids, I barely have enough money to pay my bills, and I'm at my wit's end. I am tired of people telling me, 'God has a plan. God allowed your suffering to happen for a reason.' As far as I'm concerned, I want nothing to do with God."

He told me how he had prayed desperately for his wife in her hospital bed. He'd begged God to save her life. He concluded, "Through prayer, God instantly healed our friend Jamie from a cold, but God couldn't save my wife?"

As a pastor and therapist, I felt my heart sink. This precious man, who was broken and grieving, could not turn to a loving, compassionate God for comfort. Author and speaker on religion Bruce Epperly writes:

When someone claims to be an atheist, I often reply, "Tell me about the God you don't believe in." After they describe their images of God, I typically respond, "If I thought God was like that, I'd be an atheist, too."[14]

One of the main reasons for the grieving man's inability to find comfort in God was his view of God, especially as it related to his wife's tragic passing. He believed in a God who purposed, planned, and orchestrated the traumatic events in his life. He also believed in a God who appeared to arbitrarily and instantly heal some but not others. I can understand why this man distanced himself from God.

If the person who "wins souls is wise" (Proverbs 11:30 KJV), then it is imperative from a missional and evangelistic standpoint that petitionary prayer be reimagined to make sense within a framework that includes a persuasive and love-based theodicy. The theology of the character of God needs to be stripped of extraneous negative baggage so it is not a barrier to spiritual seekers.

If we hold a view of God that causes people to cringe and distance themselves from him, then we need to make sure it is absolutely true and worth that cost. Some people get angry when they hear the proposition, "God loves everyone, even murderers." But that proposition is true and something we should declare even though some find it incomprehensible. If people cringe because they are told God picks and chooses—regardless of who prays—when to intervene and stop a child from being molested and when not to, we should challenge that theology because it is morally incomprehensible and untrue. Jesus provocatively said:

Things that cause people to stumble are bound to come, but woe to anyone through whom they come. It would be better for them to be thrown into the sea with a millstone tied around their neck than to cause one of these little ones to stumble. So watch yourselves. (Luke 17:1–3)

I am not an advocate for people drowning themselves, but I understand the hyperbole Jesus uses here. His passion was for others to experience eternal life, to come to know God profoundly, and to go out into the world spreading the good news of God's empire of love. As Christ followers, we are encouraged to be very careful that we continue Jesus's mission and do not allow outdated and primitive theology to become stumbling blocks that prevent others from coming to know and be known by God. This is precisely why petitionary prayer needs to be reimagined to make sense within a theodicy that is in line with the good and loving character of God.

PETITIONARY PRAYER AS COMMUNITY BUILDING

Let me address one last concern of petitionary prayer. Some people suggest that petitionary prayer for others is important because it can build community and communal responsibility, and that should be sufficient justification in itself. While we can applaud the secondary gains of petitionary prayer, an emphasis on the secondary benefits distracts us from vital concerns about the immature side of the spectrum. These include the failure of petitionary prayer to accomplish its primary aim: God single-handedly releasing more of his loving activity in the world.

Dutch theologian Vincent Brümmer admits, "Prayer for others is not intended to persuade God to do more for the persons prayed for than he would in his goodness have done anyway."[15] Yet Brümmer encourages the practice of petitionary prayer because it instills "responsibility and commitment toward the persons prayed for."[16] Christian philosopher Michael Murray similarly suggests that petitionary prayer "generates an interdependence among believers—one that fosters the sort of unity that God demands of the Church."[17]

I do not deny that petitionary prayer for others can have a powerful secondary effect of increasing responsibility, interdependence, and community. The mutual sharing, intimacy, sense of belonging, and subjective experience of being on a sacred mission with others and a part of a larger, transcendent purpose are priceless. But this secondary effect of petitionary prayer is often experienced and achieved without conscious knowledge.

Many years ago, I attended Wednesday-night prayer meetings at my Pentecostal church. We would pray to God for hours. We cried, shouted, pleaded, and praised, offering various kinds of petitions. We asked God to bless government leaders, save the lost, bring laborers to the church for the work of ministry, and heal the sick. Our conscious motivation as God's "warriors" was to engage in warfare prayer, hoping that through our passionate and persuasive petition we could mysteriously move God to loving action. Our praying together was not designed to bond us as a community, nor were we motivated by that desire. We were motivated principally by the belief that we were storming the gates of heaven. In other words, we believed with all sincerity that our prayers would somehow move God to accomplish the loving goals for which we were praying.

Petitionary prayer's secondary gains do not mean its primary aim should be ignored. We've discussed before that for many Christians, the chief aim of petitionary prayer is to "influence God to act in ways he would not have acted if he had not been requested to do so."[18] Many prominent authors on prayer reference this as the primary purpose for petitionary prayer. For example, E. M. Bounds, a well-known author on this topic, states:

> Prayer can lay its hand upon Almighty God and move him to do great and wonderful things.... Prayer moves men because it moves God to move men. Prayer influences men by influencing God to influence them. Prayer moves the hand that moves the world.[19]

Evangelist and licensed minister Josian Frampton writes, "Prayer unleashes God's power birthing victories, wisdom, successes and manifold blessings into lives."[20] Finally, American theologian Gregory Boyd writes:

> Prayer can save a nation (Exodus 32:10–14), and the lack of prayer can destroy it (Ezekiel 22:30). Faith-filled prayer moves God to bless, and the lack of prayer moves God to curse (2 Chronicles 30:18–20; Luke 18:1–8). Prayer can cause God to change his mind, saving cities that he had previously prophesied would be destroyed (Jeremiah 18:6–10; Jonah 3:7–10) and adding years to a person he had previously said would soon die (Isaiah 38:1–8).[21]

Such authors suggest that petitionary prayer for others is primarily meant to move God to change the world. If that is the case, does emphasizing the secondary effects of petitionary prayer mean we should ignore the primary effect? In other words, because there are benefits to petitionary prayers, such as building community, should we ignore the reality that our prayers may not make a demonstrable difference in the way God engages with the world? Should we overlook the distorted view of God held by some who pray and the superstitious elements surrounding their practice of petitionary prayer?

Let's say a religious community comes together in worship and prayer to St. Juliana, the patron saint of chronic illness, petitioning her to heal a sick member of their church. Sure, they might experience a profound sense of community and loving care among themselves afterward. But would these secondary gains justify ignoring the inherent problems with their underlying beliefs and practices in worshipping and praying to a human being instead of God?

The secondary value of petitionary prayer may be of genuine importance, but it is not the primary purpose of petitionary prayer. If we can hone the theology behind the practice, especially in relation to God's loving nature (which we will discuss in chapter six), thereby tweaking our primary aim, we can experience the optimal potential of the primary and secondary benefits. Once we've done this, petitionary prayer can put us in a unique position where we can join God in contributing to the shalom of the church and the world.

In this chapter, we've explored some of the theological pitfalls of traditionally understood petitionary prayer. In the next chapter, we will ask other important questions. Is there any evidence that this kind of prayer actually works? If it doesn't work, what are the consequences of promoting petitionary prayer? Can it paradoxically become an obstacle to shalom?

CHAPTER 4

CRITICAL EMPIRICAL AND EXPERIENTIAL CONCERNS ABOUT PETITIONARY PRAYER

In 2015, fourteen people died horrifically and twenty-two were seriously injured in the mass shooting in San Bernardino, California. In response to numerous politicians calling for prayer after the tragedy, The New York Daily News, *one of the nation's largest circulating newspapers, ran this front-page headline: "GOD ISN'T FIXING THIS."[1] The text below the headline reads, "As latest batch of innocent Americans are left lying in pools of blood, cowards who could truly end gun scourge continue to hide behind meaningless platitudes."*

An important consideration when it comes to petitionary prayer is whether it is effective. When I use the word "effective," what I mean is, does petitionary prayer accomplish what it sets out to do? Or is it a meaningless platitude? Is it clear that God is acting in the world in a way that he would not have if we hadn't prayed? Or, putting it in terms that are more measurable, is it clear that those who pray and those who are prayed for experience more shalom in the world than those who do not enact or receive prayer?

Empirical evidence regarding petitionary prayer is often used as a definitive apologetic for its practice. But, in reality, a closer scrutiny unveils a shaky evidential foundation. Ironically, petitionary prayer can even become an obstacle to the very shalom it seeks to achieve. These are the concerns this chapter will explore.

EMPIRICAL EVIDENCE OF THE BENEFITS OF PETITIONARY PRAYER

When we look at the scientific studies related to the effects of petitionary prayer, it is important to differentiate two categories of people that petitionary prayer impacts. A study could look at the impact of petitionary prayer on the *pray-ee*, or the person, event, or thing being prayed for, or it could look at the *pray-er*, the person doing the praying.

As I've stated before, the science is clear. Individualized prayer can indeed be beneficial for a person's mental, emotional, and spiritual health. A recent assessment of twenty-one clinical studies regarding the efficacy of private prayer for well-being suggests, "Frequent private prayer is associated with a significant benefit for depression, optimism, coping, and other mental health conditions such as anxiety."[2]

When the studies move from focusing on private prayer in general to focusing on the impact of petitionary prayer in particular on the pray-er, the results appear negative. This can be seen in a 2015 study that demonstrates that self-disclosure in prayers of various types has a positive relationship to well-being.[3] In other words, the more people vulnerably share their thoughts and feelings in prayer, the greater their likelihood of experiencing an increase in life satisfaction and overall emotional well-being. But, petitionary prayer rarely includes this element, though it may arise occasionally in prayers for loved ones.

Researchers also determined that frequently engaging in petitionary prayer "had a negative relationship to mental health."[4] In other words, the more people prayed petitionary prayers, the greater the likelihood that they would have mental and emotional health problems. The authors of this study suggest that petitionary prayer may have a negative relationship to mental health because it can be associated with asking for material goods and involves less introspection and meaningful self-disclosure.[5] Those who engage predominantly in petitionary prayer are typically asking God for *things*, rather than relating to him in a vulnerable way. The less people engage in an intimate relationship with God, which involves introspection and sharing one's hurts, weaknesses, and vulnerabilities, the more they may suffer mentally and emotionally.

The unique feature of one 2016 study where the pray-ers actually showed improvement using petitionary prayer was that they themselves were both the pray-er and the pray-ee. In light of the study above, prayers for the recovery of one's own health are much more likely to reveal one's thoughts and feelings about the situation. This study demonstrated that intercessory prayer was "feasible" and provided "clinically significant improvement" with dementia patients.[6]

So, what about the scientific studies examining the effects of petitionary prayer on others (the pray-ees)? Many advocates of petitionary prayer point to "the incredible research studies" that prove how beneficial it is. As a research-minded individual, I was intrigued at the prospect that petitionary prayer for others could be proven empirically and wanted to investigate this further.

If the benefits of petitionary prayer could be proved scientifically, it would certainly make sense that petitionary prayer should be engaged in more frequently to increase God's loving activity in the world. In fact, it would be selfish and sadistic *not* to pray for others. Conversely, if science proves that petitionary prayer does not work as traditionally understood, perhaps we should reconsider the practice and reimagine it in a more effective way.

Unfortunately, testing the efficacy of petitionary prayer has not been easy, and the results have not been definitive. A systematic review of seventeen studies involving petitionary prayer concludes that intercessory prayer "cannot presently be considered an empirically supported intervention for any psychological problem."[7] Therefore, according to the American Psychological Association (APA) Division 12 criteria, such prayer is considered an "experimental intervention."[8]

Some studies do offer partial support for the efficacy of petitionary prayer. A study of cancer patients from 2012 showed a "small but statistically significant improvement" in spiritual and emotional well-being among those patients who received remote intercessory prayer.[9] However, most studies indicate little or no positive benefits from this practice. The researchers conclude, "The findings are unlikely to satisfy either proponents or opponents of intercessory prayer."[10] An earlier meta-analysis—a review of fourteen research studies on intercessory prayer—concludes: "Given that the IP [intercessory prayer] literature lacks a theoretical or theological base and has failed to produce significant findings in controlled trials, we recommend that further resources not be allocated to this line of research."[11]

Some with a keen methodological eye suggest the small measurable benefit found in a handful of studies ought to be taken with a grain of salt. Dr. Richard Sloan, professor of behavioral medicine at the Columbia University Medical Center, is skeptical of the few studies that demonstrate a slightly positive effect of intercessory prayer. He writes: "Every major IP [intercessory prayer] study reporting a positive outcome has serious methodological flaws, and because of them, no evidence exists that prayer by one group of people has an effect on the health of another."[12]

One of the largest and most expensive studies of intercessory prayer to date, costing $2.4 million, was carried out by Harvard researchers and supported by the Templeton Foundation. Known as the STEP project (Study of the Therapeutic Effects of Intercessory Prayer), it examined the therapeutic effects of intercessory prayer on patients recovering from coronary artery bypass graft (CABG) surgery. The patients were randomly placed into three different groups. The members of two of the groups were told that they *may* or *may not* receive intercessory prayer, though only one of those two groups were actually to receive it. A third group was told they *would* receive prayer. Protestant and Catholic intercessors prayed for fourteen days for the participants who were designated to receive prayer. The researchers came away with two main conclusions.

> First, intercessory prayer itself had no effect on whether complications occurred after CABG. Second, patients who were certain intercessors would pray for them had a higher rate of complications than patients who were uncertain but did receive intercessory prayer.[13]

Many declared the study a $2.4 million failure. The critics and media had a field day. *Newsweek* titled one of its stories "Don't Pray for Me! Please!"[14] Firm believers in petitionary prayer for others suggested that the study didn't show favorable results because of design flaws. In other words, petitionary prayer might have been proven to be a success if the study had been properly executed. Others believed the study was doomed from the start because of all the complex variables involved in trying to prove such a hypothesis.

In addition to the questionable efficacy of prayer for individuals, there is also research suggesting that frequent prayer by a country's residents does not translate to the health of society at large. If prayer alone were powerful enough to increase God's active love in society, it would follow that one would find fewer societal ills in countries where people are praying more often. Unfortunately, that is not necessarily the case. For example, a study that looked at the frequency of prayer in fifty different countries found that in countries where people prayed more frequently, there was a "shorter life expectancy, higher infant mortality, higher violent crime, more corruption, higher abortion rates, and less peace."[15] We might conclude from this that the more societal ills a country has, the more likely the residents of that country are to pray for an improved society. More research needs to be done on the relationship between the frequency of prayer and societal problems, but this study should give us pause.

We can say a few things about the science of researching petitionary prayer and its efficacy. First, the research is clearly not definitive. There are very intelligent people on either side who will adamantly tell you, "The research says...," then go on to state their conclusion that prayer either works miraculously or doesn't work at all. But, the onus is on those who are trying to prove that petitionary prayer is empirically effective. Unfortunately, they have not effectively done so.

Second, it would be impossible to scientifically prove whether prayer is solely responsible for any given outcome because there are too many variables. While researchers try to account for extraneous variables that may influence the research, it is extremely hard to account for every variable. Who is to say that others who are not a part of the study are not praying for those same people? What about the participants' thinking patterns and how those might increase or decrease their feelings of well-being? What about the unforeseen side effects of medication? Or external stressors? How can a study account for all of these perfectly?

Third, research that proves petitionary prayer is effective would simultaneously prove God can intervene, but that he also chooses not to intervene because people do not pray. We discussed this matter earlier. Richard Sloan summarizes a scholarly critique of this interventionist God. He writes:

> It is unlikely that a god would disadvantage patients randomly assigned to a control group simply because an experimenter wanted to prove a point. Why, this criticism goes, would God intervene to cause some randomly selected patients to have a poorer course of recovery than others simply to support the hypothesis of a scientist? Do we really believe in such a capricious deity?[16]

What objective research does indicate is that petitionary prayers for others do not demonstrate mind-blowing results and that their efficacy is hard to prove. Harold Koenig, a medical doctor and director of the Center for Spirituality, Theology, and Health at Duke University, writes:

> In contrast to double-blinded distant intercessory prayer studies, which as noted above have little theological or scientific rationale, proximal person-to-person prayer and proximal intercessory prayer studies have clear theological relevance and scientific rationale (acting via plausible mind-body mechanisms).[17]

Hands-on praying, or praying for others in close proximity, is taught biblically and has been empirically proven to be effective. While being biblically encouraged, hands-off praying, or praying for others from a distance, does not have robust empirical support. In other words, from a scientific perspective, praying on behalf of others doesn't really make a difference.

PETITIONARY PRAYER AND EXPERIENTIAL CONCERNS: EVIL AND SUFFERING

We have just discussed the empirical evidence regarding petitionary prayer, but here I want to turn to discussions of experiential matters. One of the things that most motivates me to reimagine petitionary prayer is reflecting on experiential concerns, that is, the harsh reality of suffering and evil in the world. According to statistics from the United States alone, every ninety-eight seconds, someone is sexually assaulted. Annually, roughly 63,000 of those assaults involve children.[18] An estimated 16,000 murders are perpetrated each year.[19] In 2015, hate crime statistics alone include 5,850 criminal incidents and 6,885 other offenses.[20]

During the years of 2007–2011, an estimated 282,600 intentional fires were reported to fire departments, totaling $1.3 billion in property damage.[21] In 2010, there were approximately 6,185,867 larceny-thefts.[22] On a single night in January 2015, 564,708 people experienced homelessness.[23] In 2014, 47,055 deaths were attributed to drug overdoses,[24] and abuse of drugs costs an average of $700 billion annually.[25] Statistics may be numbers, but behind those numbers are the names of people and their families, who are dealing with these events and their aftermath.

Systemic injustice, suffering, and evil do not prove that petitionary prayer for others is ineffective, so what is their relevance here? For me, these statistics are evidence that the stakes are *too high to ignore*. We cannot afford to spend our time engaging in immature forms of petitionary prayer and superstitious practices.

Superstition can be defined as "an irrational, non-casual, and non-demonstrable connection between certain events, words, and actions and certain results."[26] We cannot engage in spiritual activities that cause us to feel good and think we are accomplishing great things but ultimately do not achieve the good they set out to accomplish. MacBeth writes:

> The same kinds of irrational superstitions that make us go out the same door we went in, avoid cracks in the sidewalk, or avoid the intriguing prime number 13 can haunt our prayer lives. As much as we know the difference in our heads, we often confuse prayer with magic.[27]

If people believe that praying to God in a certain manner, at a certain volume, and with certain words will convince God to single-handedly root out prejudice, reduce hate crimes, solve the problem of homelessness, heal drug addicts, stop people from committing arson, stop rapes from occurring, and so on, they are engaging in magical thinking and superstition of the worst kind. These are what I call "rabbit's foot prayers," and what Jack Corbin Getz, author of *Praying When Prayer Doesn't Work*, calls "global prayers."[28] Getz writes:

> This [superstitious praying] is when people piously entreat God to feed the hungry, shelter the homeless, or enforce world peace. While such prayers make the supplicant feel good about their investment in the world's problems, I fear their efforts are mostly futile because they pass all the responsibility for justice to God.[29]

I myself have been guilty of praying in this manner, and this does not mean that we who pray like this are not passionate, caring, and God-loving people. My aim is to examine the practice and beliefs behind petitionary prayer, not to criticize the person praying. I am suggesting that our beliefs regarding the sacred and ancient practice of prayer need to be shifted toward the mature end of the spectrum.

Petitionary prayer can become an obstacle to what the Bible refers to as shalom. Cornelius Plantinga, Jr., writes, "In the Bible, shalom means universal flourishing, wholeness, and delight…. Shalom, in other words, is the way things ought to be."[30] Petitionary prayers can become an ironic gesture. Their intent may be to increase God's loving activity and shalom in the world, but a problem arises when we pass the responsibility of shalom solely to God ("God, *you* fix the problem!"). We thereby avoid God's primary method of achieving shalom: humans, filled and led by the Spirit of God, fulfilling their vocation as God's empowered emissaries.

To understand what this entails, let's take a look at a church in New York City whose congregation had gathered for a prayer meeting. A winter storm was expected the following day, so they took time to pray for a group of homeless people who frequented an area not too far from the church: "God, pour out your love on the homeless people downtown. Help them find shelter. Protect them from the cold and from illness. Show them the salvation of your dear Son, Jesus Christ."

Perhaps those church members were the ones who needed to be saved from the pitfalls of petitionary prayer. They may have meant well, but their prayers indicated a belief that talking to God would absolve them of any responsibility to do something about the problem by placing all responsibility for resolving it upon God. Ironically, instead of being beneficial, their prayers became an obstacle to God being able to use that congregation as his Spirit-led and empowered emissaries to love, help, and save those homeless people.

God is not the one who needs to be coaxed, persuaded, or reminded in any way to love the homeless. God longs for them to be holistically saved. God grieves that some will suffer in the freezing cold. If prayer in its simplest form is an act of talking, then perhaps God whispered to that congregation: "Church, pour out your love on the homeless people downtown. Help them to find shelter. Protect them from the cold and from illness. Show them the salvation of my dear Son, Jesus." It is important not only to talk to God but also to be silent and let God talk to us. We should not see prayer as a one-sided conversation where we do the talking and God does the listening and, thus, the action. We should see prayer and the actions inspired by it as a dialogue between two parties: us and God.

My concern is that some communities who pray petitionary prayers might be guilty of what James warned us about:

> What good is it, my brothers and sisters, if someone claims to have faith but has no deeds? Can such faith save them? Suppose a brother or a sister is without clothes and daily food. If one of you says to them, "Go in peace; keep warm and well fed," but does nothing about their physical needs, what good is it? In the same way, faith by itself, if it is not accompanied by action, is dead. (James 2:14–17)

What good is it if we have prayer but no deeds, if we see brothers or sisters in Christ without clothes or food and do nothing more than pray that God will give them peace and keep them warm and well fed? What good is it if we pray for God to take care of the homeless but don't tangibly attend to their physical needs? Is petitionary prayer without action dead? Karl Barth is right when he says that prayer is "the most intimate and effective form of Christian action."[31] Nevertheless, prayer and action are two sides of the same coin. While each alone is good, when they come together, they are a potent force, contributing shalom to the world in a unique and transformative way.

Herbert and Catherine Schaible are a Christian couple who love God. In 2009, they suffered the tragic death of their two-year-old son, Kent. Kent died of untreated bacterial pneumonia. Why didn't they seek medical treatment for their son? Because they disregarded medical science and believed solely in the power of prayer. In 2013, the Schaibles were still serving a ten-year probation for neglect of their first son when their eight-month-old son, Brandon, died from treatable bacterial pneumonia. Once again, the couple had eschewed medical treatment because they believed that through prayer God would miraculously and single-handedly heal their child. The problem was that God didn't heal. Two precious children suffered needlessly and died tragic deaths.

It is easy to judge those parents for neglecting their children, but how many of us are guilty of something similar? How many times throughout our lives have we prayed fervently for those suffering and in distress, placing all the responsibility on God to answer our prayers while those for whom we prayed suffered needlessly because we took no responsibility to be part of God's answer to our prayer? How many societal ills have gone on for decades while people pray but neglect to use wisdom and take divinely inspired practical action to provide solutions? These are sobering questions.

In court, the Schaibles stated that it was God's will for their children to die. The judge refused to hear that naïve religious cliché. He said plainly, "You killed two of your children ... not God, not your church, not your religious devotion—you."[32] I wonder what heart-piercing words our just Judge has for prayerful Christians who say in the midst of tragedy, evil, and suffering, "It was God's will"?

In Matthew 25, Jesus talks about the sheep (those whose heartbeat is in sync with the rhythm of God's) and the goats (those whose heartbeat is out of sync). He surprises his audience by making a provocative claim: serving and ministering to others is serving and ministering to God. Jesus shares that God will one day separate the sheep from the goats. Their separation is not based on talking to God and professed allegiance to Christ, as both the sheep and goats call Jesus "Lord" (Matthew 25:37, 44). The separation will be made based on service and ministry to others. Jesus reveals why the goats will not have their share in the inheritance of the kingdom:

> For I was hungry and you gave me nothing to eat, I was thirsty and you gave me nothing to drink, I was a stranger and you did not invite me in, I needed clothes and you did not clothe me, I was sick and in prison and you did not look after me. (Matthew 25:42–43)

The people Jesus refers to as goats frantically ask him, "Lord, when did we see you hungry or thirsty or a stranger or needing clothes or sick or in prison, and did not help you?" (v. 44). Jesus replies, "Truly I tell you, whatever you did not do for one of the least of these, you did not do for me" (v. 45). God is so unselfishly sacrificial that his love language is to love others. To truly love God is to feed, clothe, house, and help other people in need. To not do so is to ignore and deny God.

My caution as I write this book is to make sure we are praying to and petitioning God in the right way. I don't want to be guilty of professing allegiance to Christ and praying fervently to him, believing he will take care of it all, while paradoxically denying him in the many human faces that are right before me. My heart is not to destroy petitionary prayer, chalking it up to an outdated and archaic practice. My goal is to reimagine it in a manner that allows it to come closer to its fullest potential, as we will examine more fully in the latter part of this book.

The apostle Paul writes: "When I was a child, I talked like a child, I thought like a child, I reasoned like a child. When

I became a man, I put the ways of childhood behind me" (1 Corinthians 13:11). The context of Paul's statement references spiritual gifts ceasing when we finally come face to face with who we are meant to be and the One we are meant to be with. The principle also aptly applies to an immature understanding of petitionary prayer for others. It is time for us to put away beliefs and practices that are childish and immature, especially those that are obstacles to social, spiritual, and physical justice and well-being in the world.

In order to put away childish beliefs, we need to understand what we believe and why. We must think systemically. We do not live in a one-person system made up of God alone. There is a reason why praying to God to single-handedly intervene and change the course of events does not result in change to the extent we would like to see. When exploring the topic of evil and suffering, it is critical to take other variables into account, such as economic, political, and social factors. It is important to also consider the effects of genetics, access to natural resources, laws of physics, and a host of other variables which God must cooperatively work alongside. This is not just God's story. This is *our* story, as well. This is the earth's story, the story of the entire universe and every molecule and creature, big and small. All our stories are intertwined and interconnected.

In the next chapter, we will turn to the biblical texts that are used to support the traditional model of petitionary prayer. Depending on our reading, Scripture can foster beliefs about prayer that lead us toward either ineffective or effective forms of praying on behalf of others. By using a deconstructive lens, we're also opening up the way to constructing a more intelligible and effective model of petitionary prayer in the chapters that follow.

CHAPTER 5

PETITIONARY PRAYER
AND THE BIBLE

Since I have been on this prayerful deconstructive and reconstructive journey in community, I have encountered a recurring concern: "Mark, you bring up some good questions about petitionary prayer, but even if it doesn't make sense a hundred percent, the Bible instructs us to pray for others." Common biblical texts came up repeatedly as people attempted to steer me away from my line of questioning. They would use these verses to "prove" the powerful importance of petitionary prayer and its potential as a catalyst to move God toward loving action.

Since it would take a whole book to do so, I simply cannot address every instance or insistence of petitionary prayer in the Bible. Instead, I will reflect critically on the verses and narratives that defenders of petitionary prayer most often present to me. My aim is not to offer a clear-cut vision of petitionary prayer. Rather, it is to engage in deconstructive (not destructive) strategies to locate the delicate fissures in these passages and loosen their status as definitive prooftexts of traditionally understood petitionary prayer. When applicable, I will discuss themes of theodicy and highlight views of God that are contradictory to God's loving nature, especially as demonstrated through the person of Christ.

"PRAYERS" AS WISHES

Some prayers in the Bible may be considered petitions, but a closer examination shows they would be more accurately described as wishes. Wishes are not typically addressed to God and do not have an expectation that God will intervene and actively love in a greater measure in someone's life. They are simply a way of expressing inner longings. Bible expositor Thomas Constable writes, "Communication to God constitutes prayer, but reflective statements made generally or wishes expressed to another person, even to no one in particular, are not prayers."[1] Although wishes are not prayers, because of God's love and mercy, God can take those wishes into account. If the wishes made are in accordance with God's loving will, then God, through noncoercive means and the cooperation of creaturely agents, can help bring them to pass.

One of the Greek words for the verb *pray* in the New Testament is *euchomai*. This word can also mean "to wish."[2] The context of the passage is what warrants the translation of the Greek word as *wish* rather than *pray*. Examples of *euchomai* indicating a wish are found in many passages throughout the New Testament. For example, the apostle John writes, "Dear friend, I pray [*euchomai*] that you may enjoy good health and that all may go well with you, even as your soul is getting along well" (3 John 2). John is not praying to God here that God would increase the health of Gaius and make sure everything in his life will be prosperous. John is merely engaging in a standard letter convention of the time by wishing Gaius well, which is appropriate given the health concerns frequent in antiquity.[3]

Elsewhere, the apostle Paul replies to King Agrippa, "Short time or long—I pray [*euchomai*] to God that not only you but all who are listening to me today may become what I am, except for these chains" (Acts 26:29). Although Paul says, "I pray to God," he is speaking to King Agrippa and sharing his desire that those he shares his message with can experience the same freedom in Christ he possesses.

In another passage, Paul, speaking to the Corinthians, shares his wish that they would be faithful and obedient to Christ. He writes, "Now we pray [*euchomai*] to God that you will not do anything wrong—not so that people will see that we have stood the test but so that you will do what is right even though we may seem to have failed" (2 Corinthians 13:7). When Paul says to the church at Philippi, "And this is my prayer: that your love may abound more and more in knowledge and depth of insight" (Philippians 1:9), he is expressing his wish for them to have godly insight and bear good fruit. Lastly, Paul expresses his wish for the Corinthians when he says, "We are glad whenever we are weak but you are strong; and our prayer is for your perfection" (2 Corinthians 13:9).

Wishes, as opposed to petitionary prayers directed toward God, are expressions of the heart shared with others. Paul shared his vision of what he longed to see in the believers' lives. Although wishes are not prayers, that does not mean Paul has never prayed to God concerning them. It also does not mean Paul was not prayerfully writing the wishes when he penned them. Paul and other biblical writers shared their wishes, hoping those wishes would be seeds of faith to inspire Christians toward their full potential in God.

AGONIZING AND TRAVAILING PRAYERS

Some Christians, especially within the Charismatic and Pentecostal traditions, believe those who agonize and travail in prayer in the Bible are engaging in spiritual warfare. In other words, they believe their prayers are somehow affecting and, in some mysterious way, defeating demons and the ubiquitous forces of darkness. For example, missiologist Wesley Duewel writes:

> Wrestling prayer sends mighty guided prayer missiles to destroy Satan's works.... He cannot stop prayer or escape your prayer. Press on. God's power is available and unlimited. It is released with devastating effect on Satan's forces as you militantly prevail.[4]

David Crump, professor of religion and philosophy at Calvin College, describes the mindset of a "prayer warrior" engaging in repetitive, emotionally laden, agonizing, and travailing spiritual-warfare prayer. He writes:

> The prayer warrior attacks satanic forces with a holy onslaught of continuous petition until eventually prevailing over the forces of darkness, clearing a pathway for God's unfolding purposes.[5]

However, prayers which are agonizing in nature do not demand a spiritual warfare view, especially not one where those prayers help God and angels supernaturally defeat demons. Such prayers don't motivate or move God to actively love others in a greater capacity because of their emotional depth. Prayers of this nature are rooted in a deep commitment to people or to spiritual goals. They arise organically from the depths of human beings, bursting out with tremendous passion. The intensity of these prayers could feel like war or a battle in a symbolic and metaphorical sense, but they are not literally spiritual warfare as some Christians suggest.

Jesus's prayers at Gethsemane are a perfect example of this agonizing prayer: "Abba, Father, everything is possible for you. Take this cup from me. Yet not what I will, but what you will" (Mark 14:36). In Gethsemane, Jesus shared with his heavenly

Father the depths of his sorrow, anxiety, and desire, but his prayers were not intended to change God's mind, nor did they. On the contrary, Jesus ultimately surrendered his will to God's will. Jesus knew that God's loving wisdom was going to exceed any selfishly desired outcome.

Agonizing prayers can be a powerful way to build up individuals in their faith and unite communities. They are a form of relational self-expression. But, as we've already discussed, petitioning God for others in such a fervent manner is not a more effective means of bringing forth our desired results. It is one thing to have a primary goal of sharing one's heart passionately with God, which is a beautiful and intimate endeavor. It is another to believe those energetic prayers somehow equip, move, inspire, or empower God to love someone or single-handedly change a circumstance. God typically moves upon the person or community praying and nudges them to become the Spirit-empowered answer to their own prayers.

In one of the most common verses used to encourage spiritual warfare and petitionary prayer for others, Paul writes of the agonizing prayers of Epaphras: "He is always wrestling in prayer for you, that you may stand firm in all the will of God, mature and fully assured" (Colossians 4:12). The word translated "wrestling" is the Greek *agonizomai*, which means to "struggle, to compete for a prize, fight, or labor fervently."[6]

In his Epistle to the Colossians, the apostle Paul is writing to encourage and persuade the church and to build them up in their faith. He encourages them by telling them how one of their spiritual fathers consistently prays for them. It is always refreshing to know significant people value you and take time to talk to God about you. Paul mentions Epaphras's prayers to convey the message that the Colossians are loved and cared for. He hopes to spur on faithful commitment to Christ.

Epaphras's talking with God and sharing his deep love, care, and concern for those for whom Christ poured out his blood, sweat, and tears was a beautiful act. He did what any psalmist would have done and shared his heart with God. Did Epaphras think that because of his prayer, God would intervene unilaterally, go into the Colossians' hearts, and increase the Colossians' maturity, assurance, and ability to stand firm in all the will of God? Did Epaphras think that if he didn't pray, God's active love would be diminished in the Colossians' lives? I don't believe so. For one, Paul writes a lot about immaturity and lack of spirituality among the churches to whom his letters are addressed. If all it took was fervent praying for God to unilaterally turn all those believers into mature saints, surely God would have responded to the pleas of his dedicated servants like Paul and Epaphras.

The only ones getting in the way of godly maturity were the saints at Colossae, not God. It is always God's will to increase maturity, assurance, and confidence so that we can stand firm in his will. God was already active in the Colossians' lives to the fullest extent possible and longed to increase his activity among them even more. Every inch that the door of their hearts widened was another inch through which God could enter and increase his loving, non-coercive power. The letter to the Colossians addressed spiritual needs and sought to encourage them to open the door even wider. Paul prayed, heard God's voice, and partnered with God. He wrote his letter to encourage, teach, and challenge the Colossians, and to strengthen their maturity, assurance, and ability to stand firm in all the will of God.

Furthermore, the Greek word *agonizomai* is used elsewhere in Colossians without connoting spiritual warfare. Paul writes:

> He is the one we proclaim, admonishing and teaching everyone with all wisdom, so that we may present everyone fully mature in Christ. To this end, I strenuously

contend [*agonizomai*] with all the energy Christ so powerfully works in me. (Colossians 1:28–29)

Paul uses *agonizomai* here to stress his diligent missionary labor and struggle with outside opponents who assail the
Colossians' faith, not to refer to engaging with angels and
demons. There are not two different meanings for the word in
the same letter. Due to the limited use of the word *agonizomai*
in the book of Colossians, it should be read consistently in both
occurrences.

There is no evidence that Paul and Epaphras's prayers miraculously moved or empowered God to instantaneously give the
Colossians faith and maturity. However, there is evidence that
their prayers for the Colossians burned passionately within them,
impelling them to diligently look after the Colossian believers
and minister to them as spiritual children. If petitionary prayer
were as powerful as some believe, there would be no need for
Paul and Epaphras to write a letter that urges, persuades, and
encourages the Colossians to stay on the path of righteousness.
Their prayers would have already done the job. That is what is
so significant about true, effective petitionary prayer for others.
God calls us to become the answer to those prayers that we have
asked him alone to accomplish.

Many people point to the vocative phrase in Galatians 4:19
as an example of travailing prayer: "My dear children, for whom
I am again in the pains of childbirth until Christ is formed in
you." For example, Bible teacher and radio broadcaster Derek
Prince writes:

> Paul had preached to those people and they had been
> converted. But for them to become what they needed to
> be, Paul recognized that it took more than preaching; it
> took intercessory prayer. He described that intercessory
> prayer as being "in the pains of childbirth."[7]

However, intercessory prayer is not the theme of Galatians 4:19. The words *pray, prayer, petition,* and *intercession* are not found once in the entire book of Galatians. Paul never mentions that he is praying for his readers. We can assume Paul prayed because he was passionate about prayer, but there is no direct passage in Galatians that discusses it. Paul simply uses a metaphor to describe the immense pain he feels because his spiritual children are being led astray by those preaching a false gospel. New Testament scholar Raymond Collins writes, "Paul is suffering the pains of prolonged labor because the birth of the Galatian Christians into Christ is not yet complete."[8]

Paul had a divinely inspired agenda for writing to the Galatians. He attempts to use any leverage he can to try to convince the Galatians to come back to the fold. Paul uses such an explicit metaphor to convince the Galatians how much he sincerely loves and cares for them. Any reader at the time would have felt the enormous weight of knowing they were hurting their spiritual father. Perhaps that knowledge would encourage them to do what was right and come back to Christ.

Travail, for Paul, involved thoughtful reflection, letter writing, visitation, and most certainly prayer. Mostly, it involved the excruciating emotional pain of wanting his Galatian children to become fully formed into the image of Christ. Paul travailed because the Galatians were his spiritual children on the verge of spiritual death. Until the Galatian church shed its yoke of slavery and returned to its freedom in Christ, Paul would remain in a state of labor—a state of painful yearning, hope, and anticipation for his children to be set free. Therefore, the context of the agonizing and travailing verses in Paul's letters do not necessarily point to the potency of petitionary prayer.

JAMES 5:14–18: ELIJAH'S PRAYER

While there are a number of biblical texts that seem to support the traditional understanding of petitionary prayer, we need to approach them with our understanding of the doctrine of God firmly in mind. Doing so will allow us to avoid a simplistic and literalistic reading of Scripture and instead read in light of what I call the "Quadrilateral Hermeneutic of Love." James 5:14–18, one of most oft-cited passages in the New Testament on the subject of petitionary prayer, provides us with an opportunity to explore this approach.

In James 5:14–18, James encourages the elders of the church to lay hands on and pray for the sick, the sinful, and those in need of healing prayer. He writes "The prayer of a righteous person is powerful and effective." The context is not intercessory prayer on behalf of others from a distance but prayer that is up close and personal. I am in full agreement with James: face-to-face and hand-to-hand prayer in faith is vital to the health of the church. It is petitionary prayer on behalf of others from a distance that I am seeking to reimagine.

James's appeal to Elijah's petitionary prayers for God to stop the rain for three and a half years does cause some concern. Teachers of petitionary prayer often use this reference to demonstrate its power. James writes, "Elijah was a human being like us, and he prayed fervently that it might not rain, and for three years and six months it did not rain on the earth" (James 5:17 NRSV). Does James's use of the Elijah account prove that if we pray, God will unilaterally act in the world and change lawlike regularities (laws of nature) such as naturally occurring weather patterns? Should the Elijah account be a model narrative demonstrating the power of petitionary prayer? I am not convinced.

James uses the legendary Elijah account to fit his needs. I understand some may be uncomfortable with the word "legend," or a similar word like "myth." Just mentioning those words puts me in a category of "liberal" and one who questions the inerrancy of Scripture. But I am merely trying to suggest that while Elijah was a real figure and a person of extraordinary faith, the texts written concerning him added some nuances that might not have been factually true. It is hard to believe that the ancient Israelites would not have incorporated myth and legend into their writings. They would have been the only ancient Near Eastern culture not to have done so.

The fact that some of the Elijah narrative as told by 1 and 2 Kings or retold by James may be legendary does not mean the story is not inspired by God to be in the Bible. God inspired the accounts we find in the Hebrew Bible, and he inspired James to include that account in his letter. But the fact that the text is inspired does not mean we should take everything literally, ignoring genre, metaphor, the standard practice of exaggeration, and the creative use of literary devices to communicate a message. Although not every detail happened the way it is presented in the text, this does not mean the narrative has no value and cannot inspire communal prayer or faith in God. Since the narrative is inspired enough to be part of Scripture, it is "useful for teaching, for reproof, for correction, and for training in righteousness, so that everyone who belongs to God may be proficient, equipped for every good work" (2 Timothy 3:16 NRSV). There is certainly a lot that God desires to teach us through the Elijah narrative to equip us to love and do good works for one another.

How, then, did James add to the Elijah account? First Kings 18, which details this story, does not mention "three and a half years" as James does, but only "in the third year of drought" (v.

1). Neither the text of 1 Kings 18 nor Jesus's words as recorded in the New Testament suggest that Elijah's prayers initiated the drought. James is unique in adding those details to the narrative. He probably did so to bolster his inspiring message that extraordinary faith can achieve miraculous results. Or perhaps it is simply how the story was told to him.

One of the main reasons why the account is hard to accept as evidence for petitionary prayer is the way God's character is perceived. Once again, we are back to the question of a coherent theodicy regarding a God whose nature is love. Because God's nature is love, I don't believe Elijah's prayers asking God to stop the rain for so long would have influenced God to cause harm to his creation. For the same reason, I don't believe God encouraged Elijah to pray such a prayer. Pastor and author Tony Evans writes, "Elijah's prayer didn't make God do something He hadn't intended to do, but it did reach into heaven, grab and draw down what God had already told Elijah He would do."[9] I am not sure how specifically this prayer reached into heaven, grabbed, and drew down God to do what God said he would do. That sounds confusing. I do know that a three-and-a-half-year drought would cause an enormous amount of suffering and death to plants, animals, and human beings. Jesus also mentioned the suffering and death caused by the drought (Luke 4:25). That act would demonstrate a total disregard for life on the planet, a disregard that would be at odds with the loving and uncontrolling nature of God.

Additionally, if God chose to stop the rain, God was simultaneously choosing to ignore other faithful people's desperate prayers *for* rain. God would be doing so to make a point to those whom he considered rebellious. Gregory Boyd writes:

> I submit that we dishonor God and the covenantal rela-
> tionship he forged with us on the cross if we do not assume
> that 'something else is going on' when he appears in the
> OT in ways that conflict with the nonviolent, agape-cen-
> tered character he displays on the cross.[10]

Therefore, there must be something else going on with the Elijah account. If a text portrays God in a way that is contrary to the Quadrilateral Hermeneutic of Love, the text may be portraying a culturally conditioned and immature view of God. The Quadrilateral Hermeneutic of Love is a four-part lens that gives us an accurate image of God, which all other biblical texts should be submitted to. The hermeneutic is based on the fruit of the Spirit (Galatians 5:22); the biblical definition of love (1 Corinthians 13:4–7); the only explicit parabolic picture Jesus gave of God the Father, found in the story of the Prodigal Father (Luke 15:11-31); and the radical self-giving, others-empowering life of Jesus Christ, who is the full revelation of God.

Thomas Oord aptly writes, "If love is the center of the biblical witness and the core of Christian experience, it should be the primary criterion for theology."[11] The destruction of life depicted in the Elijah account does not seem like the action of a non-violent, loving God. Is a God who wreaks havoc on the earth by causing a deadly drought in line with the characteristics of the fruit of the Spirit? Is that God in line with the compassionate, patient, loving, sin-covering father we see in the story of the Prodigal Father? Is he in line with the definition of love found in 1 Corinthians? Is he in line with who we see in the nonviolent, others-embracing Jesus? I don't think it is. Therefore, based on the Quadrilateral Hermeneutic of Love, while the text is inspired and a community of faith should wrestle with the application of the narrative, it should not be a text in which we affirm an accurate portrayal of God.

If we avoid taking the Elijah account at face value, what is really going on in this text? Boyd's Cruciform Hermeneutic gives us another plausible perspective. He details his hermeneutical approach in his massive tour de force, *The Crucifixion of the Warrior God.*[12] Since this work is composed of over fourteen-hundred pages, I can only offer a brief snapshot here.

While the Elijah account is inspired, the Old Testament writer of 1 Kings wrote from a culturally conditioned perspective. The writer had a fallen and immature concept of God. Since God does not unilaterally change people's minds and forcefully download the right image of himself into people's brains, he accommodates them in his inspiration. He therefore allowed the writer's perspective of God to remain and take on an ugly, antithetical appearance.[13]

But while the writer was culturally conditioned, that is only half of the hermeneutical story. Boyd believes that while the verses in question may represent a sub-Christlike portrait, they are still inspired. He writes, "For with the eyes of our cross-informed faith, we can discern in these literary crucifixes the same humble, stooping, self-sacrificial, sin-bearing God that we find in the historical crucifixion."[14] Verses that portray God as one who commits and commands violence are inspired not because they are factually true but because they "bear witness to God's nonviolent, self-sacrificial, enemy-loving character that was definitively revealed on Calvary."[15] God, in his patience, allowed the writer to hold to a false, projected image of him, while continuing to be a faithful covenantal partner.

Boyd makes the point that we should be honest with the text—that we should call certain passages of the Bible violent and horrific when it is necessary to do so. Indeed, it can be dangerous to leave a violent passage of Scripture unacknowledged as such. If a text represents God in a manner that is contrary to his loving, non-violent nature, it most likely came from the flawed writer's perspective and was a product of his time and culture. Interestingly, although Jesus mentions the drought, he does not attribute it to God (Luke 4:25). A violent text remains inspired because it is in the Bible, which is the Word of God in its entirety.

While sub-Christlike portraits can be horrific (such as the account of 1 Kings in which God causes a devastating drought that kills animals, vegetation, and people), they can also point to the love and fidelity of God. While human beings have always projected their worst onto God, God still came in the flesh, lived, died, and rose again for humanity and all creation. According to Boyd, horrific passages are inspired, and for those who see with eyes of faith, they point to the covenantal, unsurpassable, and, I would add, uncontrolling love of God.

Let's say the story of Elijah and his prayer is literally true. What would a biblical application of this narrative be to our everyday lives? Should we follow in Elijah's footsteps? Should we be open to praying for devastating droughts that destroy the blessedness of life in regions where people worship other gods? Should we do this to teach them a lesson so they can turn to God? That doesn't appear to be very loving and is definitely not conducive to *loving one's neighbor*.

But Elijah's miraculous feat in being able to stop and start rain merely by praying causes another concern. It encourages superstitious thinking and conveys the idea that we can change weather patterns simply by praying and having enough faith. Lawrence Richards sincerely writes, "What an example for us. If we have a prayer meeting for rain, we'd better bring an umbrella."[16] This potentially conveys an unfortunate message to the surviving family members of faithful Christians who prayed for their relatives to be saved from droughts, tsunamis, storms, and other natural disasters. Apparently, they, unlike Elijah, didn't have enough faith.

When I shared my thoughts about James with prominent pastors and teachers of prayer, I received a private response from one of them:

> I am saddened that you believe Elijah's prayer to be a fable and that you regard the inspired words of God through James the brother of Jesus to be naiveté. And saddened that James and Jesus Himself and others who revered Elijah as a man of God and a hero of the faith should be condemned to not be considered models of prayer. The crux of the matter appears to be that you do not believe the Bible to be the infallible, inspired Word of God or the events of the Bible to be true. It appears to be human intellectualism resulting in a crisis of faith.

I admire this person's faith and desire to uphold the sacredness of the biblical text. Many use the term *infallible* when they are really thinking of *inerrant*, which means "the Bible is completely truthful in all things that the biblical authors assert—whether in geographic, chronological, or theological details."[17] While I am not an inerrantist, I do believe that the Bible is the infallible Word of God. I understand that phrase differently than most people, however.

Infallible can simply mean "exempt from liability to error" or "absolutely trustworthy or sure."[18] The Bible is completely trustworthy and without error in what it is—a book full of stories, poetry, narrative, history, prophecy, apocalyptic literature, law, wisdom, metaphors, symbolism, and songs about individuals and communities relating to, and wrestling with, a holy God. The Bible is perfect. It is God's Word as it is before us. It is the messy, beautiful, and inspiring text that I, and a whole community of believers, wrestle with, which informs our faith and practice. It is also the text which, most importantly, points us to the person of Christ.

One day, as I was walking in the mall, I came across a pair of pants on a shelf looking slightly worn, with holes in them. I was astonished to discover that their price was almost two hundred dollars. Even though the pants looked worn out, they were still perfect. They were designed by their creator and co-created with manufacturers to appear that way. Those pants remind me of the biblical text. Any frayed edges, imperfections, or holes in the Bible are how God, the Master Designer, meant it to be—co-created by divine and human participation.

Although Jesus never sinned, I am sure Jesus fell as a young child learning how to walk. I can imagine Jesus accidentally hitting his hand with a carpenter's tool. We know Jesus was "tempted in every way, just as we are—yet he did not sin" (Hebrews 4:15). Therefore, as a young male, he was probably tempted with lust. We can assume Jesus got sick. It is safe to assume that Jesus on occasion became frustrated with his parents when he received rules or limits. Such instances do not imply Jesus's imperfection. Rather, they mean Jesus was not only God, he was also perfectly human. Just as Jesus is both God and man, the Bible is both inspired by God and co-constructed with humanity. It is given to us by God through the hearts, minds, and souls of fallible people. We should expect to find some frayed edges, imperfections, or holes in the biblical text because it did not fall from the heavens into someone's lap; any imperfections that are present are there because God intended them to be.

Suggesting James's Elijah account is hyperbole or legend does not mean the Bible is erroneous. I suspect James' intention was to inspire, not to give a well-thought-through, scientific, one-hundred-percent-accurate historical account. James was being pastoral, not an objective history teacher, a fact that is evidenced by his possible changing of a couple of details in the narrative. He was trying to inspire the community to prayer, especially by use of the phrase, "Elijah was a human being like us" (James 5:17).

In other words, if our spiritual heroes can pray for the miraculous and experience extraordinary results, so can we. Although inspiring, the belief that God can unilaterally intervene in the world, that he can ignore lawlike regularities that cause weather patterns to fluctuate, and that he causes catastrophic suffering to happen is not a plausible reading of the Elijah narrative. Such an interpretation is not accurately based on God's nature and does not entail practical application for modern-day believers. Therefore, while the James text should inspire us to pray, especially for one another, as the context suggests, it should not be used as proof of the power of petitionary prayer for others from a distance.

ACTS 12: THE ANGEL, THE SLEEPING SPELL, AND THE INVISIBILITY CLOAK

Defenders of petitionary prayer often point to the story of Peter's escape from prison in Acts 12:1–19. Peter's story of miraculous escape is one of the most beloved narratives to inspire hope and trust in the miracle-working power of God.

It was the night before Peter's execution. He was chained up and sleeping between two soldiers while being guarded by sixteen others. One could easily think there was no way he was getting out of this mess. Then, when all hope was lost, a bright light flashed. An angel appeared out of thin air. Instantly, Peter's heavy chains fell off. The eighteen guards appeared to be under a sleeping spell; they did not wake up, nor were they startled. Not even the guards chained to Peter were woken by the light or the jostling chains. Peter donned a cloak and walked out of the prison as if he were invisible. On his way out, a massive iron gate to the city opened without being touched. The angel disappeared, and Peter was free. Sadly, because of Peter's escape with the angel's assistance, all eighteen guards were executed at Herod's command (Acts 12:1–19).

The first problem with using this story as proof of the power of petitionary prayer is that it represents a *post hoc ergo propter hoc* logical fallacy (that is, "after this therefore because of this"). For example, let's say a friend of mine has a party outside, and it starts raining. My friend begins to pray, and five minutes later the rain stops. He says, "See, God answered my prayer." His assumption that his prayers *caused* the rain to stop is an example of *post hoc ergo propter hoc* logical fallacy.

The Bible says that "while Peter was kept in prison, the church prayed fervently to God for him" (Acts 12:5 NRSV). Granted, Luke makes a connection between prayer and Peter's release, but neither he nor we can be absolutely certain that Peter's release occurred solely because of their prayer. Correlation does not equal causation. What we do know is that they were praying and Peter was released. The church did what seemed obvious and natural in a time of persecution and crisis, which was to pray. They were still praying after Peter was released (Acts 12:12). Peter's release could very well have happened even if the church didn't pray, although, admittedly, we cannot be sure. Would God have let Peter, a chief apostle just beginning his ministry, be executed the next day because no one prayed for him? It is highly doubtful. What we do know is that Peter never gave credit to the "power of prayer"; he gave all his credit to the mighty God for his release (Acts 12:11).

The second problem relates to theodicy and takes issue with God's method of working in the world. Why is it that God is able to instantly and supernaturally send angels to break people out of prison without being seen, and yet he is unable (or unwilling) to perform miraculous acts of that nature more frequently? Why doesn't God send angels more often to prevent people, including young children, from being raped? Since God can instantly flick open a massive iron gate, why doesn't he use his power to flick a psychopathic gunman in the head before a mass murder? Why doesn't he use angels to break more innocent people out of horrific prisons? Recall that petitionary prayer for others should make sense within a coherent theodicy. A God who can send angels to stop evil and open gates without touching them but does not perform similar miraculous events to reduce evil more often is problematic.

Lastly, there is the issue of historicity. There are well-respected New Testament scholars who suggest that the miraculous account of Peter's prison break was not so miraculous. Although many Christians have pointed me to this narrative to prove the power of petitionary prayer to move God to interfere in the world unilaterally, a closer inspection brings the potency of this text into question. Conservative scholar I. Howard Marshall writes in his commentary on Acts:

> The story is plainly regarded by the narrator as miraculous at every point. It can be argued that it is a legend, especially since several motifs in the story can be paralleled from other ancient stories, some of which would have been current knowledge in the first century, and it can be claimed that in a world of such superstitions it would be only natural for Christians to believe that their God could do the same kind of things as other deities. On this view, a story of a release from prison by human agencies may have acquired legendary features in the course of telling. It is impossible to prove either way.[19]

Some scholars suggest that legends of angels, bright lights, and prison escapes were a common literary motif at the time of Luke's writing. In other words, creative writers at that time intentionally used these motifs to add greater importance to characters and events in their stories. Therefore, it is possible that while there was an actual historical account of Peter's escape from prison with help from an insider, the account later evolved into something more spectacular. New Testament scholar Richard Longenecker writes, "Stories about prison doors opening of their own accord and of miraculous escapes from imprisonment were popular in the ancient world, and the form of such legends undoubtedly influenced to some extent Luke's narrative here."[20]

Similarly, biblical scholar F. F. Bruce writes:

> There are some features of the narrative that would point to a carefully planned and skillfully executed "inside job"; probably that was Agrippa's conclusion. There are other features which are strongly reminiscent of the "form" in which other miraculous escapes from prison are described in ancient literature.[21]

With a different emphasis, renowned theologian John Stott suggests that we should not expect to perform miracles like Jesus and makes a brief comment on the Lukan prison escape. Although Stott does not argue against the literality of the narrative, he writes, "We should not, therefore, expect to do [miracles] ourselves today. Nor should we expect to be miraculously rescued from prison by the angel of the Lord."[22]

While the commentators I have cited focus on the narrative as legend or point to the cessation of miraculous events, there are others who focus on the story's unique meaning in its historical, political, and religious context. For example, John B. Weaver highlights the political function embedded in the Lukan narrative. He writes:

From the Classical period into Late Antiquity, the god's liberation of devotees from prison furthered the cult's introduction into a city. Similarly, in Acts, the miraculous opening of the jail represents God's counterblow to the suppression of the gospel by civic authorities. This is partly communicated by the symbolism of the physical structure of the prison, which in Acts represents the power of indigenous leaders to restrain God's emissaries. The breaking of the prison thus signifies the breaking of resistant authority.[23]

Furthermore, Josep Rius-Camps and Jenny Read-Heimerdinger suggest that the Lukan account was not miraculous, as depicted, but was masterfully crafted and creatively written to make a subtle theological connection between Peter's release and the Exodus of Israel. They write:

In this central sequence, it will emerge that just as Yahweh delivered his people from the oppression of Egypt, so now, in this night of messianic expectation, he will deliver Peter from the oppression of the Jews, indeed from the system of Jewish regulations and expectations that held him prisoner. The application is nothing less shocking for, with the message that the Jews have become the enemy of the people of God, the original roles in the Exodus have been turned upside down.[24]

Although Peter's escape from prison was a historical account, perhaps F. F. Bruce's suggestion was right: it was an "inside job" and did not occur fantastically as is depicted in the Lukan narrative. It does not necessarily follow that Luke fabricated the event; perhaps when Luke received the account, that is what was told to him.

As I have argued in this chapter, the fact that some stories in Scripture may have taken on legendary elements does not strip them of their inspired nature or their usefulness "for teaching, for reproof, and for training in righteousness." The biggest take-away from the passage is that God is to be praised. Indeed, the chapter concludes with Herod being killed because he "did not give praise to God" (Acts 12:23).

God did something incredible for Peter. If it was an inside job, how beautiful it was for an amazing God to inspire and empower someone on the inside to cooperate with him to save and release the world-changing apostle Peter. Just when Jesus's disciples thought Peter was as good as dead, God made a way of escape. That is miraculous indeed!

With regard to prayer, the church believed they were going to lose their leader and companion in faith. Luke's account is a beautiful portrayal of a community coming together to pray and share their grief-stricken hearts with God. While sharing our hearts with God and one another *is* beautiful and sacred, we should be cautious before using the narrative to demonstrate the power of petitionary prayer. We should be careful not to say, "See, if you just pray and petition God, miracles will happen. God will use supernatural angels, sleeping spells, and invisibility cloaks to set your loved ones free."

DANIEL 10: SPIRITUAL WARFARE

The book of Daniel is apocalyptic literature laced with proph-ecy, numerology, dreams, visions, definitive portrayals of good and evil, and detailed eschatology. Noncanonical apocalyptic literature, which was common at the time of Daniel's writing, had similar elements. Apocalyptic literature employs exaggera-tive, metaphorical, and metaphysical language. It uses creative narrative events to veil contemporary flesh-and-blood historical events.

Daniel 10 is best viewed as the work of a creative spiritual poet who was trying to make sense of the chaos and suffering he saw all around him and within his community rather than as the work of an empirically minded historian trying to accurately portray a spiritual realm. While early readers of Daniel could decode some of Daniel's messages, the meaning and referents became more obscure over time.[25] Apocalyptic scholar John Collins reminds us:

> Biblical scholarship in general has suffered from a preoccupation with the referential aspects of language and with the factual information that can be extracted from a text. Such an attitude is especially detrimental to the study of poetic and mythological material, which is expressive language, articulating feelings and attitudes rather than describing reality in an objective way. The apocalyptic literature provides a rather clear example of language that is expressive rather than referential, symbolic rather than factual.[26]

Biblical scholar Stephen Cook cautions against a reductionist approach to apocalyptic literature, especially one that suggests it is *just* conveying truths about historical matters. He writes, "Too often interpreters mistake the blazing, mammoth characters of apocalyptic narratives for colorful expressions of the routine and commonplace—for persons, places, or events within human experience and history."[27] In other words, Cook cautions against suggesting apocalyptic literature is just referring to historical events and has nothing to do with spiritual truths and a metaphysical realm.

While apocalyptic literature may be trying to convey *both* historical and metaphysical truths, the meanings are veiled by a creative literary genre. Due to the ambiguous metaphysical truths embedded within the apocalyptic texts, the texts should not be mined too quickly for universal applications to prayer.

It is unwise to understand Daniel 10 to be making a definitive theological claim that there are times when the answer to our prayers could take weeks to arrive because angels and demons are having epic battles in the heavenly realm. The same caution should be used in making a theological claim that Daniel 10 definitively demonstrates that intercessory prayer is a powerful form of spiritual warfare. The text does not demonstrate the notion that our prayers are synergistically affecting the outcome of angelic warfare while simultaneously affecting earthly circumstances.

We don't know why we have a story about angels and princes fighting and delaying the answer to Daniel's prayer for over twenty-one days. It is in our sacred text, therefore it is inspired. Because we do not know the reason for its inclusion in Scripture, we wrestle with the questions of how it came about and what it means for us today. Perhaps the skillful, creative, and prophetic writer of this apocalyptic literature had an imagination like that of Christian fantasy novelist C. S. Lewis. The genre of apocalyptic literature was his God-inspired outlet to convey contemporary, traumatic, and dramatic truth.

Apocalyptic writers commonly used visions and angels as literary devices to signify the divine importance of the information conveyed. I can imagine a community reading this text and saying to themselves, "A mighty angel leaving a battle to deliver a message! Wow, this message must be vitally important. We had better heed this." What we definitely know is that Daniel intentionally uses a nonliteral, creative, and strategic writing style, just like other non-biblical, apocalyptic writers in his day.

Let's say those events depicted by the author of Daniel were real. God does not need angels to deliver visions, he can deliver them himself and without delay (Genesis 15:1; 46:2; Isaiah 1:1; Ezekiel 11:24; Acts 16:9). As a matter of fact, early on in the book, God gives Daniel a vision at night based on a prayer Daniel had prayed that morning (2:19). Talk about express shipping! In the chapter before the events in question (Daniel 10), when Daniel is "still in prayer" (9:21), Gabriel comes to him straightaway, saying, "As soon as you began to pray, an answer was given, which I have come to tell you, for you are highly esteemed" (9:23). Why does it take the angel twenty-one days to come to Daniel when God could give the vision himself or send another angel to come to him promptly, as Gabriel does?

Whoever the Prince of Persia is, at the time of the messenger's visit to Daniel, the messenger and the archangel Michael have not yet defeated him. The angel talking to Daniel tells him he will go back to fight the Prince of Persia. Therefore, the Prince of Persia is still alive, well, and fighting in battle while they are talking. The angel says to Daniel, "Soon I will return to fight against the prince of Persia, and when I go, the prince of Greece will come" (Daniel 10:20). Why would it take that long for an archangel and other angels to defeat the Prince of Persia? One assumes an archangel or "chief prince" (10:13) is much more powerful than other angels. Additionally, it is highly doubtful that a powerful and influential angel would leave a fierce battle to give Daniel a non-urgent vision ("the vision concerns a time yet to come," 10:14) before returning immediately to battle. This is especially true when God could have given Daniel an immediate vision, something that God had done for him many times in the past.

Apocalyptic literature does not have to be free from plot holes. This genre intentionally incorporates visions, angels, demons, and symbolism as literary devices to disclose more earthy truths.[28] The question of exactly what mysteries Daniel was trying to convey behind his symbolism has led to a myriad of interpretations and hundreds of books. They are conversations that are outside of our particular focus on prayer.

While God does use angels to deliver messages on occasion, God is an omnipresent being who can, and does, promptly answer prayers, speak to us, and show us visions. I would think a proper theology of prayer—especially one developed under the New Covenant—would not have us worrying about whether our mail will get stuck in transit due to the heavenly postal workers' fighting with each other. Our understanding of God's transcendence and immanence is different than that of the Old Testament writers. We don't believe God hangs out in the heavens and occasionally comes to earth for important tasks. Modern-day believers believe in God's transcendence, but they focus more on his immanent closeness, that is, his dwelling within us via the Holy Spirit. Do you think demons battling outside of us can keep God from speaking a message to us when he is inside us, especially if we are humbly open to hearing his voice? Because God is inside us, it doesn't take long for the mail to arrive.

As an aside, if there have been angels battling demons for hundreds of thousands of years, shouldn't we assume that there are many dead angels and demons? Considering angels are on 'Team God,' and God is a brilliant war strategist with enormous power, one wonders how 'Team Satan' has not been annihilated after all this time. Some say angels and demons can't die. If that is the case, what are their weapons? If they cannot die, how big are the stakes? If they cannot presently be annihilated, then why aren't most of them rounded up and placed in chains until their final swim in the lake of fire (Matthew 25:41; Revelation 20)? I am not suggesting that angels and demons do not exist. I am merely saying that there are a lot of unanswered questions about their roles, their weaknesses, their battle strategies, and the inter-play between our world and theirs.

Let's get back to prayer. We have no indication whatsoever that Daniel was engaged in any "spiritual warfare." God heard Daniel the very first time he prayed: "Since the first day that you set your mind to gain understanding and to humble yourself before your God, your words were heard, and I have come in response to them" (10:12). God's hearing after one prayer gives credence to Jesus's words when he says, "And when you pray, do not keep on babbling like pagans, for they think they will be heard because of their many words" (Matthew 6:7).

Unlike in Daniel 9, where Daniel is "in prayer and petition, in fasting, and in sackcloth" (v. 3), in Daniel 10, he is said to have "mourned" and fasted for three weeks. That is not to say Daniel did not pray and petition, only that Daniel 10 doesn't make any mention of it, nor does the chapter make use of the word "prayer." Perhaps Daniel was exhausted and was literally in a state of helplessness and mourning, as the text suggests. The messen-ger tells Daniel, "The prince of the Persian kingdom resisted me twenty-one days" (10:13). We have no indication that Daniel's mourning contributed anything to the battle between the mes-senger, Michael, and the Prince of Persia. Therefore, Daniel 10 should not be viewed as a text proving the success of petitionary prayer and spiritual warfare.

MATTHEW 8 AND LUKE 7: HEALING THE CENTURION'S SERVANT

One of the clearest accounts of petitionary prayer on behalf of others is found in Matthew 8 and Luke 7. A centurion, who typically would have been a Roman soldier in charge of eighty to a hundred men, has a paralyzed servant who is sick and on the verge of dying. The centurion asks Jesus to heal his servant without going to his home to be physically near the man. The centurion believes that just as he is a man of authority and can speak a word and soldiers under him will obey, Jesus, a man of spiritual authority, can speak a word and instantly heal the centurion's servant. Jesus turns to the crowd and says, "'I tell you, I have not found such great faith even in Israel.' Then the men who had been sent returned to the house and found the servant well" (Luke 7:9–10).

What can we say about petitionary prayer from Jesus's healing of the centurion's servant? First, Jesus's healing loved ones at a distance at the request of others is a rare occurrence. Evangelical New Testament scholar Craig Evans suggests that the healing of an official's son found in John 4:45–54 is another account of the centurion's servant being healed as found in Matthew 8 and Luke 7,[29] which leaves us with only one other additional case of distance-healing, that of the Canaanite's daughter (Matthew 15:22–28). Therefore, there are just two occasions when this kind of healing happens. Certainly Jesus could have performed similar healings on other occasions, but we are unaware of any other instances.

Second, and related to the first point, Jesus gives us a hint of his preferred method of healing. When the centurion asks Jesus to heal his servant, Jesus asks, "Shall I come and heal him?" (Matthew 8:7). Jesus's first course of action is to go to the home, be in proximity to the servant, and heal him there. Jesus performs the majority of healings close to those he meets on his journey and close to those who come to him.

Perhaps the men who took the paralytic to see Jesus in Luke 5:17–26 (par. Matthew 9:1–8; Mark 2:1–12) knew about Jesus's preferred method of healing. They may have thought it would be better for their friend to personally see Jesus than to simply ask him to heal their friend at home. They probably based their actions on the majority of reports they had heard about Jesus. They may have felt so strongly that their friend should see Jesus personally that "they went up on the roof and lowered him on his mat through the tiles into the middle of the crowd, right in front of Jesus" (Luke 5:19). While the Bible says that Jesus healed people from a distance based on the petitions of others, his question in Matthew 8:7 seems to imply that he prefers being face to face. The overwhelming evidence in the Bible points to the need for people to individually open their hearts, minds, and bodies for Jesus to heal them. Perhaps praying for others on their behalf does not allow the people being prayed for to open their hearts to receive God's grace in the moment.

Third, we cannot assume Jesus heals the servant unilaterally without the cooperation of the servant. The centurion is a man of great faith. Since he is friends with Jewish elders, he is most likely a God-fearing gentile who has a relationship with God. He has such a good reputation with the Jews that the elders say to Jesus, "This man deserves to have you do this, because he loves our nation and has built our synagogue" (Luke 7:4–5). High praise indeed! Because the centurion is close with God and also appears to be close to his servant, it is likely that the servant has a relationship with God too. In Luke's account, Jesus is on his way to the centurion's home to heal the servant but is stopped on the way by the centurion's friends, who tell Jesus that the centurion believes he is not worthy to have Jesus enter his home (Luke 7:6). Since the centurion knew Jesus was coming, we can assume that the servant must have been aware too and that he must have demonstrated faith. In the moment Jesus said the healing word, the servant who was open to healing cooperated with God and therefore experienced a miraculous recovery.

Fourth, navigating the text pastorally and using this narrative as a prooftext for the power of petitionary prayers for others is challenging. Jesus says of the centurion, "I have not found such great faith even in Israel." Jesus states that the centurion's faith is greater than that of any one of the thousands upon thousands of Jewish people in Israel. If that kind of extraordinary faith is a pre-requisite for God to heal on our behalf, then who could achieve it?

Additionally, do we say to Christians that others who are paralyzed, sick, and dying could be healed if they had enough humility and faith? Those who use the narrative as a prooftext must go all the way with this line of reasoning. When we pray for family members who are sick and in the throes of death and they remain unhealed, at least some of the time it must be because of our lack of amazing faith. If we want to take the text literally and teach on petitionary prayer, I don't know how one could avoid shaming Christians. How easy it could be for someone to say, "My sister died from the flu because I didn't have enough faith."

Furthermore, how do pastors properly teach their congre-gants to become mature enough to have the kind of faith to petition God to instantly heal sick and dying friends and family? If it is biblical, should we encourage people by giving them prac-tical steps to reach that pinnacle of faith? Is that really possible?

Lastly, the gospel writer includes the story of the centurion and his servant to make a point other than that petitionary prayer for others is powerful. The writer had a God-inspired agenda. He wanted to encourage readers to place their faith in the miracle-working Jesus, the Messiah, who has power and authority over sickness and death. Also, by including the story in his gospel, the author sought to prove that believing gentiles had a seat at the end-time banquet table of salvation but that unbelieving and faithless Jews did not.[30] This would have been quite a provocative message for Jews at the time of Jesus.

CONCLUSION

Godly and well-respected pastors, teachers, and authors have shared biblical texts with me that they believe prove that the traditional understanding of petitionary prayer is biblical, real, and ordained by God to accomplish God's will. Forming a theology of petitionary prayer for others based on Scripture requires that we work through some hermeneutical issues. It requires that we separate wishes from prayers. It requires that we separate myth, legend, and metaphorical and symbolic literature from objective history. It requires that we separate event descriptions (this is what happened) from biblical prescriptions (this is what you should do). It also requires us to ask, when faced with verses that offer images of God that are contrary to the person and character of Christ and the definition of love, "What else is going on?" These are not easy tasks.

While I have not carried out an exegesis of each passage in detail, I have attempted to deconstruct the most relevant texts. My intent has been to loosen the grip of a reductionist, literal view and free them from their use as prooftexts for the traditional understanding of petitionary prayer. I don't want to merely *deconstruct* petitionary prayer for others but also to *reconstruct* petitionary prayer in a way that prioritizes God's Word, as well as integrating reason, experience, and tradition. In the next chapter, I invite you to reflect on God's character and the way he chooses to interact with all of these variables. We will begin to construct a coherent theodicy that will help us to develop a more mature model of petitionary prayer, one in which we can fully take part in our story with God.

PART 3

RECONSTRUCTION

See Pg 124

CHAPTER 6

GOD'S PERFECT, UNCONTROLLING LOVE

Petitionary prayer is susceptible to a great many pitfalls. Yet it also has the power to effect profound change. In fact, when the theology that shapes our practice of petitionary prayer is expanded to include a view that prioritizes God's uncontrolling, loving nature, it is one of the most potent types of prayer.

In this chapter, we will explore God's perfect, wise, intimate, and uncontrolling love in light of Thomas Oord's theodicy of essential kenosis. The theoretical foundation that we lay in this chapter will set the stage for us to see how God's love interacts with human free will and other dynamics within his creation. This will also prepare us for further explorations into the articulation of a more coherent, mature, and practical model of petitionary prayer, which will be discussed in future chapters.

GOD'S PERFECT UNCONTROLLING LOVE

In the Gospel of Matthew, Jesus tells his disciples and other curious spiritual seekers to "Love your enemies and pray for those who persecute you, that you may be children of your Father in heaven" (Matthew 5:44–45). What Jesus asks people to do here appears irrational, absurd, and against our natural inclinations. We normally reserve our love for friends and family, and we withhold it from our enemies; indeed, our enemies could be described as the people we categorically do not love.

In telling his listeners to love their enemies, Jesus is asking them to love like God, who "causes his sun to rise on the evil and the good, and sends rain on the righteous and the unrighteous" (Matthew 5:45b). Jesus goes on to say, "Be perfect, therefore, as your heavenly Father is perfect" (Matthew 5:48). In other words, we are to emulate God's perfect, unconditional, all-inclusive love. God demonstrates perfect love by loving those who do not love him back: his prayer-less enemies.

We do not pray God's nature into existence. God's perfect love extends to all, without the necessity of prayer. The birds do not pray, but a loving God takes care of them (Matthew 6:26). The lilies do not intercede, yet God is mindful of them (Matthew 6:28). Enemies and persecutors of God do not pray, but God loves them (Matthew 5:43–48; Luke 6:27). The ungrateful and wicked do not pray, yet God is kind to them (Luke 6:35). God "so loved the world" without the prompting of prayer (John 3:16). God exists as who he is: a God of love. God's attributes—his holiness, justice, mercy, and power—are funneled through that love.

Recently, I spoke to a professor and well-known speaker on the topic of prayer. He quoted John Wesley, who said, "God does nothing except in response to believing prayer."[1] I asked him why atheists in, say, predominantly atheistic countries like China or Denmark experience the same "miracles" as praying Christians experience. Why are they shocked to find their cancer has unexpectedly gone into remission? Why do they receive money as a gift at the last minute to pay rent? Why do they find true love, recover from addictions, find great parking spots, reconcile with estranged family members, and recover from depression? In other words, if "God does nothing except in response to believing prayer," then why do atheists experience many of the things Christians pray for, except without the prayer?

His answer? "They were lucky."

Although randomness is a dynamic that exists in the world and opens up space for creativity and novelty to arise, I do not believe that all the good that atheists and the irreligious experience is due to simple 'luck'. Rather, it is due to God's generous, universal, and non-prejudicial love. Speaking of the ubiquitous and inclusive love of the Holy Spirit, Anglican priest and theologian Norman Pittinger writes:

> The Holy Spirit is not confined to the ecclesiastical community but is operative in the cosmos, in human history, and in every person—above all, in all response to whatever is known of God as he seeks unfailingly to disclose and give himself to his human children.[2]

Saying "God is love" is not pure sentimentality pushed by a liberal and progressive agenda. God *is* love; it is biblical (1 John 4:8, 16). If God is love, then the biblical definition of love (1 Corinthians 13:4–8) must also be characteristic of God. Therefore, God is patient and kind. God does not envy or boast. God is not arrogant or rude. God does not insist on his own way. God is not irritable or resentful. God does not rejoice at wrongdoing but rejoices with the truth. God bears all things, believes all things, hopes all things, endures all things.

Further, if the *fruit* of the Spirit is "love, joy, peace, forbearance, kindness, goodness, faithfulness, gentleness and self-control" (Galatians 5:22–23), then the Spirit's own character must reflect that fruit. Therefore, God is loving, joyful, peaceful, patient, kind, good, faithful, gentle, and self-controlled. God is the epitome of love and is always loving because that is what

God is and that is what he does. God is never passive but is always in motion, loving to his fullest extent while respecting our free will and other agencies in the process.

God is always the smartest, wisest, most loving, and most personable agent in the room. He knows how to love better than anyone. He is an expert, a virtuoso. God always serenades the universe through his Spirit and captivates those who lend an ear. God's love is trustworthy; it never fails. Every moment pulsates with the love of God. If my dad is sick, then I can rest assured that God is lovingly and compassionately doing the best he can to heal him within an array of vast complexities and agencies (one of which is my dad's free will).

Conspiring prayer (discussed further in chapters eight and nine) takes seriously the profound truth that "In him we live and move and have our being" (Acts 17:28). God is deeply immanent—that is, profoundly close—and intimate. God does not step into time and intervene on occasion only when we pray fervently for him to do so. He is always close, always moving, always on mission, always loving, calling, challenging, encouraging, comforting, and convicting, moment to moment. Saint Patrick, who lived in the fifth century, is Ireland's patron saint and one of its most famous missionaries. He had remarkable insight into the immanence of Christ. Here is an excerpt from one of his prayers:

Christ with me, Christ before me,

Christ behind me,

Christ in me, Christ beneath me,

Christ above me,

Christ on my right, Christ on my left,

Christ when I lie down, Christ when I sit,

Christ when I stand,

Christ in the heart of everyone who thinks of me,

Christ in the mouth of everyone who speaks of me,

Christ in every eye that sees me,

Christ in every ear that hears me.

Amen.

God's close, intimate presence is also attested by other writers. Irish philosopher and theologian Peter Rollins talks about God's "hyper-presence."[3] Rollins gives the analogy of a sunken ship deep in the ocean. He writes: "While the ship contains the water and the water contains the ship, the ship only contains a fraction of the water while the water contains the whole of the ship."[4] God is so hyper-present that we can become blind to what he is doing, unable to appreciate the hyper-saturation of beauty and grace all around us.

The key is to become what professor of theology and church historian Leonard Sweet calls a "semiotician," or "one who can read the signs."[5] He writes: "Our quest is to be so filled with the Spirit of God, and to be wearing interpretive Jesus goggles, that we not only notice, but are able to interpret and respond."[6]

May we have the power, together with all God's holy people, to grasp "how wide and long and high and deep is the love of Christ" (Ephesians 3:18), and to realize that God's active love is everywhere. We only need to put on our "Jesus goggles" to become more aware of that love, which is all around us.

God's active love is not only perfect, wise, and intimate. It is also uncontrolling.[7] God's uncontrolling love is an essential feature of the persuasive theodicy Thomas Jay Oord calls "essential kenosis."[8] Oord describes essential kenosis and details God's primary manner of working in the world:

The model of God as essentially kenotic says God's eternal nature is uncontrolling love. Because of love, God necessarily provides freedom/agency to creatures, and God works by empowering and inspiring creation toward well-being. God also necessarily upholds the regularities of the universe because those regularities derive from God's eternal nature of love. Randomness in the world and creaturely free will are genuine, and God is not a dictator mysteriously pulling the strings. God never controls others. But God sometimes acts miraculously, in noncoercive ways. God providentially guides and calls all creation toward love and beauty.[9]

God's love precludes God from unilaterally controlling others. In other words, it is not that God chooses not to, it is that God *cannot* disregard the free will and agency of people and force his way into situations to change the outcome. God's uncontrolling and loving nature vastly shapes his manner of working in the world.

GOD IS NOT IN CONTROL

Today, as we are bombarded with horrific stories and shocking images all day long, the overwhelming evidence of evil creates an enormous amount of cognitive dissonance that demands a verdict. The idea of a Blueprint God, who is sovereignly in control of all things like a Grand Puppet Master, is untenable.

I hypothesize that Christians who believe in a God who is not only in complete control, but who, in his sovereign will, has planned out in advance all the events that will ever occur in our lives, would not be able to maintain this position if they were forced to watch on a screen all the evil taking place worldwide in any given one-hour period of time. Granted, an experiment of that nature would probably cause the person to go insane or, at the very least, to be scarred for life. Assuming they could maintain their sanity, it is highly unlikely they could continue to hold so firmly to the belief that all things occur according to God's loving will and intricately mapped-out plan.

When we get past the Christian platitudes, if we take the risk of facing the chaos that unfolds before us on a daily basis, and if we reflect on the nature of prayer, it becomes apparent that many questions remain. Philip Yancey quotes an inquisitive philosophy professor, with whom he had communicated about the nature of both evil and prayer:

> If God can influence the course of events, then a God who is willing to cure colds and provide parking spaces but is not willing to prevent Auschwitz and Hiroshima is morally repugnant. Since Hiroshima and Auschwitz did occur, one must infer that God cannot (or has a policy never to) influence the course of worldly events.[10]

Oord's model of essential kenosis helps us understand that we should not imagine that God was unwilling to influence the course of horrific events, such as Auschwitz and Hiroshima. Rather, we should recognize that the character of God's powerful love is self-giving, others-empowering, uncontrolling, and noncoercive.[11] Oord writes: "Because love is the preeminent and necessary attribute in God's nature, God cannot withdraw, override or fail to provide the freedom, agency, self-organizing and lawlike regularity God gives. Divine love limits divine power."[12]

God's uncontrolling love defines what he can and cannot do. And, contrary to popular belief, there are indeed some things God cannot do, as Scripture itself teaches. God cannot lie (Hebrews 6:18); he cannot be tempted (James 1:13); he cannot be prejudiced (Acts 10:34–35); he cannot sin (Deuteronomy 32:4); and he cannot get tired (Isaiah 40:28).

And God cannot unilaterally control people and events. It is not that God did not want to stop the events at Auschwitz and Hiroshima. It is that God simply could not control the people and lawlike regularities involved in those events to stop them from occurring. Theologian Thomas G. Belt reminds us:

> We can know that for any given evil, God, being perfectly loving, always does all God can do to maximize good and minimize evil, but we also know that given the metaphysics of freedom and risk, how much good God is able to actualize on any given occasion is conditioned by these creational factors.[13]

It is not that God can control creatures but chooses not to do so. It is that God cannot control creatures due to his loving nature.[14] Simply put, love does not control. Therefore, God does not unilaterally control others—hence the term *uncontrolling love* used by Oord and throughout this very book. God is doing all he can do to maximize good and minimize evil, but God is constrained by his uncontrolling, loving nature. Love preserves the sanctity of free will even at the cost of what that will may freely choose. To disregard and usurp free will is to cease loving.

Oord writes, "Mermaids cannot run marathons because a mermaid's nature includes leglessness. God cannot create controllable creatures because God's nature is uncontrolling love."[15] Mermaids may be mythical creatures, but the analogy holds truth. A mermaid running would be as contradictory as God controlling others and unilaterally causing events to occur. God is so loving that to control or manipulate others would be to defy his own character. For God to control is a logical, moral, and metaphysical impossibility.

Suggesting God *cannot* unilaterally control people or events and manipulate them as God sees fit is of huge theological significance. Many Christians do not hold to this idea because of a reluctance to imply that God is not powerful enough to do so. For example, the Christian philosopher William Hasker states one common perspective: "God's capacity to control the detailed course of events is limited only by his self-restraint, not by any inability to do so."[16] In other words, many Christians believe God can control but chooses not to. We have already seen how this view of God is problematic because a God who can unilaterally stop evil but who instead exercises "self-restraint" is a God who may be morally culpable. It is a complete paradigm shift to suggest that God simply *cannot* control because of his uncontrolling, loving nature.

Oord makes a compelling case that in addition to God being unable to control people, God's agency is in relationship with other variables, such as randomness, creaturely agency, and lawlike regularities (e.g. the law of gravity, the law of thermodynamics, weather systems, etc.). It is not that God allows evil or horrific events to occur. Rather, it is impossible for God to control people and events, and therefore all kinds of free creatures, randomness, and lawlike regularities run amok, sometimes in the direction of beauty and other times in the direction of destruction. Evil events occur precisely because a loving and uncontrolling God cannot control all things.

The Shack is a well-known novel by William Paul Young that has also been adapted into a movie. Young's book was written out of his own experiences of pain and trauma, including sexual abuse. Though it is fiction, it is full of meaty theological reflections. The book centers around a man named Mack Philips. Mack struggles with the question of why God, who is supposed to be good, allowed his daughter to be kidnapped and murdered in a shack in the mountains. God, or "Papa," who appears in the form of an African-American woman, responds to Mack's pain and burning questions in the very shack where his daughter was killed. Papa says:

> She didn't have to, Mackenzie. This was no plan of Papa's. Papa has never needed evil to accomplish his good purposes. It is you humans who have embraced evil and Papa has responded with goodness. What happened to Missy was the work of evil and no one in your world is immune from it.[17]

God did not write a detailed script, puppeteering Mack and his family's entire narrative to perfection—or anyone else's for that matter. It was not God's will for Mack's daughter to be randomly chosen and murdered. You would naturally find evil and suffering running rampant in a world where God is not in control. Much of the evil that we see and experience in the world comes from human choices that are not bathed in beauty, goodness, and truth. Horrific events also occur because randomness, lawlike regularities, and human choices collide.

For many, humans having agency and free will to make choices in the world makes sense. Bad things happen because people choose to do terrible things. But randomness and lawlike regularities are seldom discussed. Understanding their interaction in everyday events helps us to understand further the complexities involved in human suffering. Understanding God's inability to control randomness and lawlike regularities helps us understand why some tragic events occur.

Randomness, or what William Hasker calls "chanciness,"[18] and lawlike regularities, such as Newton's laws of motion and gravity, culminate in what can be called freak accidents. After performing a simple Google search, I found a few examples of freak accidents that occurred in the United States in the month during which this was written. An elderly man was driving a car in California when a baseball-sized plumbing nut came through his windshield, hit him in the neck, and instantly killed him. A young man was at the gym when the weights slipped from his grip and fell on him; he died from internal injuries. A former NFL player and philanthropist died when he slipped and fell while playing catch with his son during a family vacation. A man was hunting in Louisiana when a bullet ricocheted off his target, hit him in the chest and killed him. A sixty-two-year-old woman was driving in her beach buggy when her long scarf got trapped in her rear wheel and choked her to death.

Randomness and lawlike regularities are a part of life. They are built into the fabric of our existence and can bring about positive, neutral, or—as these stories demonstrate—negative events. God can influence events, and by doing so does help to avoid many tragedies from occurring, but God cannot unilaterally control them, not even to avoid senseless and tragic accidents.

Randomness and lawlike regularities exist because they contribute to potentiality. Anything can, and does, happen. Randomness and potentiality invite the possibility of phenomena such as growth, decay, movement, and the experiences of choice, joy, despair, connection, and disconnection. They ensure that nothing remains the same and everything is fluid. A world created without the possibility of randomness and potential would lack life and luster. It would be a one-dimensional world full of static impassable forms without growth, movement, or fluidity. It would be like a beautifully dull yet immortal and never-aging painting, forever sitting in a dingy, forgotten attic. It exists, but it is stuck in time and lifeless.

A world without potentiality is not the kind of world we want to live in. Therefore, "time and chance" (Ecclesiastes 9:11) are important for the beautiful messiness and zestiness of life. Time and chance bring forth novelty, spontaneity, promotions, new connections, and epic adventures. They also bring forth tragic accidents, suffering, and death, which God has no control over.

We often pray, "Your kingdom come, your will be done, on earth as it is in heaven" (Matthew 6:10). It doesn't make sense to pray for God's kingdom to come and his will to be done if God's reign is already everywhere and his will is always done on earth. Yet Jesus calls us to pray that way because there are choices, events, and outcomes that are contrary to God's good and gracious will. Whether through God's volition or, as I have argued, due to God's uncontrolling, loving nature, most theologians admit that God does not unilaterally control people or the circumstances in which they live.

THE BEST OF ALL POSSIBLE WORLDS

Although the idea of God not being in control can be scary, perhaps such a world is the best possible world and the only one where the highest ideals of love, goodness, and beauty can be achieved. Kenneth Pak writes:

> God must do that which is consistent with his nature. And his nature demands that, if he creates a world, he creates one with the highest intrinsic and extrinsic goodness or value. Such a world involves creatures with genuine freedom, with great virtues in it. And genuine freedom, if it is to be real, cannot be unilaterally coerced.[19]

The atheist philosopher Jean-Paul Sartre knew that love is love no longer when it controls or coerces others. Sartre writes: "The man who wants to be loved does not desire the enslavement of the beloved. He is not bent on becoming the object of passion which flows forth mechanically. He does not want to possess an automaton."[20]

God's perfect, uncontrolling, and non-coercive love shaped the world he would create. Therefore, God could not create a world full of robots. To create a world where love is the highest good, God took risks and created people and other entities with genuine freedom.

What kind of world would we live in if there were no possibility of choice, pain, and evil? Would we experience less of what we consider beautiful and good as a consequence of living in such a world? Kevin Moore suggests we live in a world where there are "evil-dependent goods."[21] In other words, there are goods that only come about because of the possibility of sin, suffering, and evil. Moore lists examples such as "various sorts of compassion, clemency, gracious forgiveness, mercy, reconciliation, redemption, adoption, sacrificial love, and the forbearing and overcoming of temptation."[22] Some of the most valued human experiences exist precisely because of the possibility of choice, sin, suffering, and evil.

That some valued and good experiences come from evil does not mean God relishes evil. Scripture makes it clear that "love does not delight in evil" (1 Corinthians 13:6). While our world may be the best of all possible worlds, that does not mean God created the world because evil-dependent goods would exist at their optimal level. God's motivation was not to create evil. God created out of love and took creative risks, and the by-product happened to be experiences we value highly in the face of evil. Many of the songs we call "oldies but goodies," the timeless movies we consider classics, and the inspiring stories we tell one another are typically created in the aftermath of suffering and evil. Of course, love too is all the sweeter when one considers that it has been a choice and has not been forced.

As much as we yearn for God to unilaterally control people like Professor X from the Marvel Universe and forcefully stop people from committing acts of evil, he simply cannot. We wish God would ignore free will on occasion and knock a rapist unconscious as he is about to engage in a violent transgression, but it is simply outside the bounds of what God can do. God can't stop evil like a divine Whack-A-Mole. God also can't disregard lawlike regularities and stop a tsunami from killing hundreds of thousands of innocent people. The kind of world where God intervenes unilaterally is a different kind of world altogether. It would be a world possessing less intrinsic and extrinsic goodness and value.

A plausible theodicy must have God's nature and character at its front and center. Now that we have explored God's perfect, uncontrolling love, let's address the question of what God's uncontrolling love means for the world he has created and for us as prayerful agents of change.

CHAPTER 7

GOD'S OPEN-DOOR POLICY

While God's essential kenosis and uncontrolling love are consistent with a coherent theodicy and help to provide the answers to many of the major questions about the presence of evil in the world, they are likely to raise new questions for Christians who are acquainted with traditional models of God's sovereignty and petitionary prayer. Specifically, how can a God who does not control or coerce act lovingly within his creation? It's all well and good that God has a loving will, but how can he be expected to accomplish his will in the midst of creaturely freedom?

In this chapter, we will propose an answer to that question by exploring how God's love interacts with human free will and other dynamics within his creation, such as randomness and lawlike regularities. How we understand God's manner of working in the world will set the foundation for the practical application of prayer, which chapters eight and nine will explore.

GOD'S OPEN-DOOR POLICY

Throughout history, doors have been used as metaphors to signify various things: new opportunities ("The door opened for me to get that new promotion!"), the end of one's options ("The door of opportunity closed on that new investment"), passageways into epic fairy-tale lands (C. S. Lewis's *The Lion, the Witch and the Wardrobe*), and strange portals into parallel universes (*Monsters, Inc.*). We also have a front door to our hearts.[1]

Jesus said, "Here I am! I stand at the door and knock. If anyone hears my voice and opens the door, I will come in and eat with that person, and they with me" (Revelation 3:20). It was not a literal door that Jesus referred to but a symbolic door to the human heart. The door is the way to the innermost part of who we are—the inner sanctum where our mind, will, and emotions reside.

As previously discussed, one of the pitfalls of the traditional model of petitionary prayer is that it tends to ask God to love or change others without taking into consideration other dynamics and agencies, such as a person's free will. Conspiring prayer, however, takes free will and a coherent theodicy into perspective. God has a greater chance of changing those who open the doors of their hearts and surrender their wills to his because God cannot control others.

Jesus says, "Ask and it will be given to you; seek and you will find; knock and the door will be opened to you" (Matthew 7:7; Luke 11:9). Notice Jesus did not say, "It will be given to you and those you pray for," or "Seek and *they* will find," or "Knock and the door will be opened to *them*." More often than not, the gifts of God come to the asker, to the seeker, and to the one who opens the door (i.e. "Your faith has healed you," Luke 18:42).

Why? It is those who open their hearts to God who can become willing recipients of his loving action. While God blesses all people and creation through common grace, a deeper measure of God's grace and the gifts he can bestow is experienced by the person who willfully says "yes" to God. The Bible says, "And without faith it is impossible to please God, because anyone who comes to him must believe that he exists and that he rewards those who earnestly seek him" (Hebrews 11:6).

God experiences enormous pleasure when anyone comes to him in faith, intentionally assenting to God's presence and believing his nature is to reward those who seek him. That is why we are encouraged to "draw near to God with a sincere heart and with the full assurance that faith brings" (Hebrews 10:22). James also writes, "Come near to God and he will come near to you" (4:8). Water running down a mountain wets everything on its surface, but it is the most porous of rocks and vegetation where the water can find a deep place to dwell and nourish life. The one who intentionally draws near to the always-near God receives the greater reward.

Petitionary prayer for others cannot contradict spiritual lawlike regularities. For example, one spiritual lawlike regularity is that God cannot force his way into places where there are "Do Not Enter" signs. A person without faith or openness to God's presence limits what God can do in their lives. If a person pushes God away, then no matter how much one may pray for them, God is kept from loving more fully. James reminds his audience that a person who doubts "should not expect to receive anything from the Lord" (1:7). It is not that God doesn't want to give gifts and blessings to that person, but God has an open-door policy. God's love does not control and only enters fully when people willfully open their door to him; God doesn't force doors open.

We want to live in a world where there is less inequality, prejudice, and racism, and so does God. God does all he can to help us achieve these basic aims, but he cannot control people. People's hearts must be open to receive God's grace in order to root out our tendencies to judge, marginalize, and oppress others. I want to live in a world where people don't blow themselves up with the intention of killing large amounts of innocent people. Guess what? God wants the same thing. But God will not intervene unilaterally, bypassing the will of people in a controlling manner to root out hatred and oppressive tendencies, even if we petition and plead with him to do so.

Just because God is not in *unilateral* control, however, does not mean God is unable to exercise any kind of control at all. God is not passive and powerless. According to the Oxford dictionary, the word *control* can mean "the power to influence or direct people's behaviour or the course of events."[2] I suggest God lovingly and powerfully influences us by inviting, empowering, inspiring, filling, convicting, leading, comforting, healing, and challenging us toward ever-increasing experiences of shalom. While many people experience God's active love without realizing it, God's influence can become magnified with individuals who have "ears to hear" (Mark 4:9; Luke 8:8) and who open their hearts in faith.

Jesus was an incredible miracle worker. He taught in synagogues with authority and power. He was God incarnate, the Creator of the world manifested in the flesh. Yet, despite his power, even Jesus was limited. Mark 6:5–6 states, "He could not do any miracles there, except lay his hands on a few sick people and heal them. He was amazed at their lack of faith." Can you imagine? Jesus, the all-powerful, mighty God, met people he couldn't heal? It certainly had nothing to do with Jesus's desire or power.

It is important to point out that we should not blame all unanswered prayer on lack of faith, because that would be cruel. There are too many Christians who are bogged down by the weight of shame because they look at others who are healed and ask, "Why not me?" They conclude something is wrong with their faith, their prayer life, or themselves as people.

What helps is to understand that human agency is not the only agency that God is in relationship to. There are other doors that need to be open for God to accomplish creative relational endeavors. Oord states:

> The organisms, body parts, organs and cells of our bodies can resist God's offer of new forms of life that involve healing. These creaturely elements and organisms have agency too, and this agency can sometimes thwart miracles. Even when we consciously say yes in faith to the divine desire for our well-being, our bodies may not cooperate with God's healing plans.[3]

A person's unfortunate choice to keep the door of their heart closed to God, while paramount, is only one dynamic among many that prevent blessings from flowing in, and through, our lives. This is one of the benefits of holding a view of God's uncontrolling love. It is not that God can heal, save, and deliver, but chooses not to. God's love precludes him from overriding the agency of elements, organisms, lawlike regularities, and the will of human beings.

God always performs the most loving acts possible in every moment in every nook and cranny of existence. God can be trusted completely because he would never purposefully or maliciously harm any person, especially not for some grand Machiavellian purpose. This way of thinking about God, alongside an understanding of God's relationship to human free will and other agencies, is a grand proclamation. Keeping God's faithful and uncontrolling love in mind radically changes how we think about prayer.

"BASIC NEEDS" AND "DISCRETIONARY NEEDS"

Does God's perfect, wise, intimate, and uncontrolling love imply that petitionary prayer can never change God's mind? Do petitionary prayers ever make a difference, altering God's loving direction? David Basinger's distinction between "basic needs" and "discretionary needs" is helpful for our discussion.[4] Basinger defines basic needs as those that will "keep our long-term quality of life—our long-term physical and mental well-being—from being diminished significantly" and discretionary needs as those needs that will "simply enhance our quality of life."[5] While there can definitely be overlap between the two terms and they should not be considered in a formulaic manner, they are helpful for our discussion of petitionary prayer.

DISCRETIONARY NEEDS

Here, I want to look at discretionary needs, but rather than looking at those things that will enhance "our" quality of life, I want to expand the conversation and consider praying for discretionary needs for others also (i.e., "God, please give my son the Ferrari he wants"). While God is always desiring and actively seeking to bring forth the basic needs of others for whom we pray, God does not always provide for discretionary needs. But God does, on occasion, help contribute to the potential of our desires coming to fruition.

Since we are in a loving relationship with God and share with him the loving aspirations we have for other people, he may hear our prayers and change his actions toward a new divine aim. It is true that God's knowledge of all the dynamics involved is vastly superior to our own. Since God knows what would maximally contribute to a person's well-being, God has a particular will for those we pray for. But God is also deeply relational. God empathizes with the desires of our hearts. God is willing to consider our prayers and possibly grant requests because of them. Of course, God is also free to lovingly say "no" and continue to woo us toward his perfect will.

For example, a man named John sends an email to his friends: "Can you pray for me that I get this new job in Colorado?" John's request is a discretionary prayer, this time on his own behalf, and it is not about basic spiritual, physical, mental, and emotional needs for his overall well-being. He already has an excellent job but prefers to live next to a few friends of his. Since God knows all that can be presently known, God has the preferred aim of John taking a promotion in Ohio. God knows John could thrive there. John would meet new people in Ohio who would enliven his faith. The Ohio location would also be an optimal place for John to increase his influence and expand the kingdom of God's love in vital and unique ways. John is set on Colorado. He passionately and consistently prays to God and invites his friends and family to pray that God will open the door for him get the job there.

First, John would be better off if he prayed for God's loving will to be done and followed God's wise leading. Sure, it's easy to go where one might feel most safe and comfortable, but God doesn't always call us to what feels safe and comfortable. Second, John deviating from God's primary aim does not mean God can't accommodate and continue to journey with him and have new loving aims for him. Chris Band uses the illustration of a GPS:

> If we choose to ignore the directions and deviate from the ideal route, it doesn't switch itself off in disgust but recalculates the journey to find the new route, starting from our

current location. In the same way, God doesn't write us off or force us out of the driving seat when, ignoring him, we steer our own way through life. He takes us on from where we are.[6]

God may take John's prayers and desires and those of his family and friends into account. God may then decide to nudge a few receptive hearts that can co-open the door of opportunity for John. God, in cooperation with others, may answer John's prayer and help him receive the job in Colorado. Or he may not.

Prayers for others' discretionary needs are viable. We are in a relationship with a God who loves us and those for whom we pray. God having an ultimate loving aim in mind does not mean God is inflexible and unable to be moved. God is a moveable mover. Being in a relationship means there is a push and pull, a dialogical dance of mutual influence. Therefore, we can change God. We cannot change God's nature, but we can change his direction. We can change God's mind because we are in a relationship with him, just as God can change ours.

The prophet Jeremiah admitted the possibility that God would change his mind when he preached repentance to the Judeans: "Now therefore amend your ways and your doings, and obey the voice of the LORD your God, and the LORD will change his mind about the disaster that he has pronounced against you" (Jeremiah 26:13 NRSV).[7] Some believers will cite Balaam's divine oracle to Balak as proof that God cannot change his mind. The oracle reads, "God is not human, that he should lie, not a human being, that he should change his mind" (Numbers 23:19a). They usually stop there. But the continuation of the oracle clarifies the context in which God does not change his mind: "Does he speak and then not act? Does he promise and not fulfill?" (Numbers 23:19b). It is only in relation to his promises that he does not change his mind. In other words, God does not break his promises.

Not only does the Bible talk about the possibility of God changing his mind, it describes several instances where he does just that. After Aaron made the golden calf and the Israelites offered sacrifices to it while Moses was on the mountain, God decided to destroy them. Moses' dialogue with God (his petitionary prayer for them) caused God to change his mind: "And the LORD changed his mind about the disaster that he planned to bring on his people" (Exodus 32:14 NRSV). Similarly, in the story of Jonah, the repentant behavior of the Ninevites changed God's mind about overthrowing their city. "When God saw what they did, how they turned from their evil ways, God changed his mind about the calamity that he had said he would bring upon them; and he did not do it" (Jonah 3:10 NRSV). These are not cases where God had made a promise, as Balaam was talking about, but cases where God had planned a course of action.

BASIC NEEDS

Praying for discretionary needs is different from praying for basic needs, which are the types of prayers emphasized in this book. Basic needs are needs for God to love, heal, save, and deliver from the most fundamental obstacles to human flourishing. For example, a basic need is to be free from poverty. God never desires that people be deprived of sustenance and starve to death. Another basic need is to be free from racism and oppression. It is never God's will for people to suffer discrimination because of the way they look, for example, or because of their gender, sexual orientation, race, and so on. Other basic needs include the necessity of a world free from violence and genocide and a world in which healing from devastating injuries and accidents can occur. A basic spiritual need is one of salvation. God always desires people to be saved and to know his love intimately.

Babies do not need to ask a parent to clothe them. Children do not need to ask parents to take care of them when they are sick. They don't need to ask parents to protect them from predators. Parents clothe, love, and protect children because they are attuned to their children's needs and love accordingly. They do so without their children asking or pleading for them to do so. While Jesus encourages us to pray, "Give us today our daily bread" (Matthew 6:11), this prayer is a symbol of our dependence on the God who always desires to freely provide our basic needs. It is an implicit acknowledgement that God is the ultimate source of the fulfillment of those most basic needs. Asking for our needs to be met opens us up in the moment to receiving God's freely available graces in their various forms.

God always seeks to lovingly meet the basic needs of humanity and the rest of his creation. Moment to moment, God offers pathways to meet those needs. God's primary medium for providing for basic needs is people. Remember, God has an open-door policy. God continually looks for open-hearted faith on the earth and seeks the cooperation of human beings to co-steward creation toward shalom. While the motivation to pray common, petitionary prayers for the basic needs of others is pure, God is already actively seeking to meet those needs. God isn't keeping us from shalom; *we* are, or those other agencies we have no control over are.

OPEN BUT SKEPTICAL

While I am skeptical that praying for the basic needs of others increases God's unilateral, loving activity in the world, I am in the minority. Certainly, those who hold to a traditional notion of God's power believe God can do anything at any time, regardless of the circumstances or people's will. Many nontraditional authors and teachers of prayer who hold to belief in a loving, non-coercive, and uncontrolling God also believe that petitionary prayer increases God's active love and provision for basic needs. Bruce Epperly, for example, writes: "Our prayers open us and others to greater movements, possibilities, and energies of transformation in the God-world relationship, specifically involving those situations for whom I pray."[8]

In her discussion of intercessory prayer, author and professor of theology Marjorie Suchocki writes: "[Prayer] changes what God can offer…. releasing more of the divine resources toward the good that God can then use…. Praying for another's well-being allows God to weave us into the other's well-being."[9]

Kathleen Fischer, author on spirituality and faith, writes that our prayers "insert new love and strength into the situation of the person we are praying for, and they are received by God and become a real factor in God's ongoing guidance of the world."[10]

Finally, theologian and minister Philip Clements-Jewery writes: "God thus uses our prayers for others to make available to them an aim that has a stronger likelihood of being accepted and actualized by them than would be the case if the prayer had not been made, although they remain free to realize or not realize the aim."[11]

While I am sympathetic to these views, I simply do not have enough faith to wholeheartedly trust them. I am doubtful that talking to the wisest, most powerful, and most loving God will increase his unilateral provision and power to supply for the basic needs of others. I am open to the possibility, but, for many reasons, the otherworldly nature of these theopoetics is not convincing.

A friend of mine on Facebook once asked her friends to pray for her family. She posted, "Can you pray that God would comfort my brother and his wife? They lost their child and are in desperate need of God's grace." It is hard to believe that praying alone in one's room, "God, please comfort her friends and extend your loving mercy and grace to that family," would increase God's comfort, mercy, and grace in their lives. God doesn't wait for us to pray before he begins comforting his children who are grieving. God doesn't say, "The fifth person finally prayed for me to extend grace and mercy, so now I am finally willing to do so."

Praying to God that he would comfort and pour out his grace on my friend's family is like asking my wife to do the dishes while she is in the middle of doing the dishes. It is better to ask God, "How can I join you in extending your comfort and grace to them?" just as it is better to ask my wife, "Hey, honey, can I help you with that?"

Let me illustrate my concern about praying for others' basic needs with one more story about a rambunctious seven-year-old named Shane, who was in need of his parent's loving care. A friendly neighbor was watching Shane one day after school while his parents were at work. Her own son and Shane were in the back yard, playing on the swings. Fooling around and swinging dangerously high, Shane fell off the swing. As a consequence, he scraped his arm badly, bruised his leg, and was filthy from the damp dirt.

When the neighbor called to explain what had happened, Shane's mom asked if the neighbor had called her husband yet. Yes, the neighbor replied, but her husband was not answering his phone. Shane's mom then called her husband, but couldn't reach him either. A self-described helicopter mom, she drove frantically to the neighbor's house, which was thirty minutes away. While driving, she called her husband again. He finally answered, and she anxiously told him the situation.

"He fell and hurt his leg and arm," she said. "I hope he is okay. Where are you? Are you close to him? Please, if you get there first, take care of him. Okay?"

The husband told her calmly, "I am with Shane. I'm taking care of him. I know you're upset. I know you're concerned. It will be okay. I'm cleaning him up right now. I'll see you when you get here, and we can take care of him together." The mother arrived ten minutes later and helped her husband take care of Shane.

When Shane's mother spoke to her husband on the phone, did she relay any information to him that he did not already know? No. Did she share information with him that helped him take care of their son? No. Did her information inspire him, move him, motivate him, or empower him to actively love Shane more? No. Did her husband lovingly listen to his wife? Yes. Did her husband share her concern? Yes. Did her husband appreciate his wife's help when she arrived? Yes.

God cherishes our desire to talk with him about loved ones who are hurting. God loves when we join him in what he is doing in the world. It signifies trust. It shows that we value our relationship with him, that we are God-reliant as opposed to self-reliant. On the other hand, to share our concerns believing they will increase God's motivation and power to love, heal, and comfort is wishful thinking.

God invites us to contemplate the full ramifications of what it means to believe God is love. Love is relational and invites intimacy, openness, and communication. That relationship invites changes in God and in ourselves. But praying does not change God's loving nature. God as love is always loving and will continue to love, seeking the shalom of all creation without our prayers to make him do so.

As poetic and inspiring as it is to talk about "energies of transformation" or "releasing more of the divine resources" and to declare that prayers "insert new love and strength into the situation," it is hard to believe that prayer increases God's loving activity to fulfill basic needs. The apostles once said to Jesus, "Increase our faith" (Luke 17:5). That is exactly what I pray in regard to other's basic needs. I am open and prayerful, but skeptical.

And I am skeptical for the many reasons that I have already mentioned. I don't see the theological claims of Epperly, Suchocki, Fischer, Clements-Jewery, and others backed up by lived experience. Their view of prayer suggests that more prayer means more of God's healing and transformational love while less prayer means less of God's healing and transformational love. On that theological premise, a person with the flu being prayed for by one thousand people in a megachurch should recover at a faster rate than another person with the flu with similar contextual variables being prayed for by ten people in a smaller church. I don't think prayer and the God we pray to work that way.

Even if we buy into quantum mechanics, which many contemporary practitioners of prayer emphasize, and we accept that weird things happen on a subatomic level; even if we hold that consciousness is not bound by our tiny brains and we are all interconnected and entangled in some vast web of energetic consciousness; even if we believe these things, there is no substantial evidence that thoughts, spoken or unspoken, can affect the outcome of events in any demonstrable way. When it comes to natural disasters, social injustice, and loved ones in crises, even if "prayer works," since its workings are most likely small and slow, *sending good thoughts* or talking to God (prayer) may not be all that is needed to bring forth a greater degree of shalom. The immediacy of many dire situations demands more than what the snail's pace butterfly effect of good intentions, loving vibes, and ten-second prayers can offer.

Would a person's tears falling into a vast ocean make the water wetter? Would they increase the power of the ocean's currents? Would the tears increase the mass and volume of the ocean? Perhaps; perhaps not. If they did, the extent would be minuscule. Praying to God for intimacy's sake is deeply rewarding. Both God and we are mutually enriched as we experience the delight of a heart-to-heart connection. It is doubtful that praying to God and believing that our prayers are effective in increasing the vastness of God's loving power and his capacity to change other people and events in our shalom-starved world will actually make them so.

If prayer changes God and increases God's energetic force of love toward people and circumstances, why didn't the cumulative force of millions of Jews and other believers in God who prayed and cried out to God for mercy keep them from being tortured and executed in the Holocaust? If prayer does not positively and clearly increase God's effects, how much energy, new love, and divine provision are really infused into people's lives? If research studies or lived experience do not decisively demonstrate robust differences, how can people make such definitive theological claims regarding how God works in the world?

I am also skeptical because of the underlying mechanics of these thinkers' theological proposals. For example, Clements-Jewery writes that God's loving aim for others has "a stronger likelihood of being accepted and actualized" if they are prayed for.[12] But how can praying for others make their wills more malleable and able to receive God's graces? It certainly cannot be done apart from God's activity. Therefore, in their view, prayer must be an act that affects God. According to their implicit theology, God can make the prayed-for person more open to receiving God's loving will. We have already seen how problematic that thinking can be. God can't single-handedly control people's wills. If God could make someone's will more malleable to receive God's healing graces, wouldn't God have done so already?

Various theologians that champion God's uncontrolling love have an underlying assumption regarding the mechanics of prayer and its ability to increase God's provision for basic needs. They believe God feels what we feel in prayer and is therefore changed because of our prayers. God is changed by the experience to such an extent that it increases God's loving energy and activity toward fulfilling people's basic needs. They believe our prayers change God and then expand his loving energies of transformation into the lives of the people we are praying for.

Is this accurate, or is it wishful thinking? How does talking to God change God in this way? It assumes that God's ability to feel the depths of the prayerful person's experience necessitates an increase in God's active love. I can see how this might happen with people, but it is difficult to comprehend when it comes to God.

One day, while watching television, I saw starving children in pain. They were desperately yearning for a mouthful of food. A passionate spokesperson came on the screen asking for money. My heart strings were pulled. The experience moved me, and I felt a greater urgency to help fulfill their request. On another occasion, I was with parents who pleaded for therapeutic support for their struggling children. I felt their hurt and desperation. I cried with them. Their suffering moved me to want to help them. Witnessing the suffering of others and hearing their stories can change us. It can stir us toward loving compassion and increase our loving action. However, we can't assume that God has a similar experience with us when we pray.

Certainly our experiences and passionate prayers move God deeply. God changes in the sense of experiencing fully the present moment. Our pain becomes God's pain. Our cares become God's cares. But does God's feeling what we feel increase God's loving activity in the world?

Unlike God, I was not aware of the children's hunger or the family's plight. Therefore, I did not help them until after I found out about their anguish. God knows all and always performs the most loving act possible in every moment. God knows our requests before we ask them. God is already present with the person or situation we are praying for and loves them in ways we cannot comprehend.

God might feel our pain and desperation while praying for another, but that does not mean our prayers inform him of something he didn't know beforehand. God's empathy does not mean that our prayers are like gasoline, fueling the fire of God's love, making it hotter and spreading it further. God is not like a reluctant superhero who holds back his superpower of love until something tragic happens, which then causes him to fully embrace his loving, non-coercive power and moves him to lovingly save the day. Our prayers move God because God is relational. That our prayers motivate God or somehow expand his love in the lives of those who are desperate for shalom is something I struggle to believe.

Part of my skepticism regarding the power of petitionary prayer for meeting basic needs is not based on God's character but on dynamics and agencies outside of his control. The gap between the vision of shalom that people are praying for and the undesirable circumstance they or others experience is not due to God's lack of loving desire or activity. While God always loves to the greatest extent possible, God is not in control of everything and everybody. God needs open doors. God has chosen to work alongside other entities and agencies in the world, such as people, randomness, and lawlike regularities, to accomplish his will.[13]

In the next chapter, we will begin to establish what it means to pray petitionary prayers in line with the theodicy I have proposed in the last two chapters. Petitionary prayer must be considered in light of God's perfect, uncontrolling love. It should also be considered in view of God's open-door policy. God needs open-hearted people who have willing hands to accomplish his liberating purposes on the earth.

CHAPTER 8

PRACTICAL PRINCIPLES FOR CONSPIRING PRAYER

Understanding God's nature and God's desire to work through the open-doors of human hearts provides a foundation for a coherent theodicy. This theodicy sets the stage for the next set of principles, which focus on the practical application of petitionary prayer. I call this proposed model for petitionary prayer "conspiring prayer." The English word *conspire* comes from the Latin word *conspirare*, which literally means "to breathe together" and figuratively "to act in harmony toward a common end."[1] In today's usage, the word conspire has a negative connotation, which is to plot with someone to do something wrong or evil; but conspiring prayer combines both of the former meanings.

Conspiring prayer is performed *with* God rather than *to* God. Conspiring prayer is a form of prayer where we create space in our busy lives to align our hearts with God's heart, where our spirit and God's Spirit breathe harmoniously together, and where we plot together to subversively overcome evil with acts of love and goodness (Romans 12:21). This subversive, sacred practice calls forth thankful, open-hearted listeners who humbly petition and partner with God to become divine echoes, committed to bring forth shalom in the world. Let's take a look at how conspiring prayer differs from the typical understanding of petitionary prayer.

PRAYING WITH THE UNCONTROLLING GOD OF LOVE

One of the main differences between less effective petitionary prayer and conspiring prayer is that the former is petition *to* God. Those who petition God in this way ask him to unilaterally intervene in people's lives or the world. They tend to deem God as the sole agent of change. Petitions *to* God, particularly in their most immature form, can be likened to rubbing a magic rabbit's foot. The petitioner believes that if they pray hard enough and with the right words along with the right behavior, God will, without any cooperation from other agencies, instantly fulfill the request.

In contrast, conspiring prayer shares petitions *with* God. It is not a monologue, like praying for God to unilaterally love in concrete ways in the world. Rather, it is a collaborative dialogue, a friendship, a two-way street, an intimate dance between lovers. We share with God our joys, hopes, and grief about the present reality and our loving vision of what could be, and God shares his with us.

Conspiring petitions are also a test of true intimacy that uncovers our core motive: do we seek intimacy (relationship) or utility (goods for prayers rendered) with God? Jewish philosopher Martin Buber differentiates between intimate, sacrificial, and relational prayer and utility prayer, or what he prefers to call "magic." Buber writes:

> Magic wants to be effective without entering into any relationship and performs its arts in the void, while sacrifice and prayer step "before the countenance" into the perfection of the sacred basic word that signifies reciprocity. They say You [God] and listen.[2]

A person praying magical prayers is devoid of a relational focus. That person is concerned about what they can receive and sees God as an object or a dispensary of goods. God may as well be a genie in a lamp. According to Buber, true sacrificial prayer requires relationship and reciprocity. Those who pray mature prayers acknowledge God as personable, with a subjective core different from one's own. They acknowledge that there is a "You" (God) and an "I" in prayer and, therefore, a sacred "us." Conspiring prayer is relational at its core.

We need to ask ourselves, however, if we would still pray to God and share our heartfelt request if we knew that he couldn't single-handedly control events and instantly give us what we wanted. Our honest answer shines a light on our primary motive in prayer. It is possible that some people's prayer lives would radically diminish once they realized God is not the all-powerful deity who can instantly make things happen in the world. Some would prefer to treat prayer as a 'drive-thru window' where they can place their order quickly and one-sidedly, without much engagement with the other party, rather than as an intimate meal in which both parties set the table and cook the food together. If we are honest, for many of us prayer can be a mixed bag. However, the goal is to increase our experiential understanding of God as a relatable subject and not as an object to be used.

When we pray conspiring prayers, we pray prayers that are in alignment with God's uncontrolling and loving character. We know that God is loving and good, therefore, we do not pray God's love and goodness into being. God's love is a verb and is always up to something. God is not waiting for people to pray so that he can act all alone, come down from heaven, and stop evil in its tracks when beckoned. The conspiring prayer model assumes God is doing all he can do in every moment to provide for the basic needs of those we are praying for.

Keeping God's loving character in mind gives us the confidence to pray with him regarding the vision of love, beauty, justice, and peace we all desire in the world. Therefore, we may still pray, "God, my heart longs for you to pour out your love on my dad," or, "God, this violence has to stop! I long for you to bring justice to those who have tragically lost their lives," while believing God loves to his greatest ability in every moment. But these prayers would be prayed with a different motivation and understanding of how God works in the world. They are not meant to get God to instantly do something loving and just. They are meant simply to share our hearts with God. We know he hears the requests, values them, feels the need with us, and is longing to meet that need, particularly if those prayers are in alignment with his own loving will (1 John 5:14). Shalom is a collaborative and co-lingering effort.

When praying conspiring prayers, we groan with God. The groaning we experience is the outcome of the mysterious links between God's Spirit and our spirits. Romans 8:26–27 says:

> In the same way, the Spirit helps us in our weakness. We do not know what we ought to pray for, but the Spirit himself intercedes for us through wordless groans. And he who searches our hearts knows the mind of the Spirit, because the Spirit intercedes for God's people in accordance with the will of God.

When our hearts are aligned, we long for what God longs for. We grieve what God grieves. There are times when we—including God—are doing all we can for a person or a situation and the only thing left to do is to share our grief with one another. John Stott writes: "The Holy Spirit identifies with our groans, with the pain of the world and the church, and shares in the longing for the final freedom of both. We and he groan together."[3]

When we are in touch with the suffering and needs of others and we are in tune with the Spirit, our prayers, birthed from the groaning within, are God's prayers for the world. When we pray according to the will and love of God, we can rest assured it is God's desire to work together toward that aim. We become God's "co-workers in God's service" (1 Corinthians 3:9).

God doesn't need to be reminded of the people and places still devoid of the liberation of the kingdom of God, but we do. The same yearning for love, healing, and justice we feel is felt by God, only exponentially more so. We seek to trust that God is good all the time and all the time he is good. When we do so, we realize that our desires, if they are under the umbrella of love, are God's desires, too. Prayers for basic needs such as more love, more peace, less violence, healing from injury or illness, salvation, the eradication of hunger and poverty, and the healing of our planet are already a "Yes and Amen" to God.

Churches all over the world are praying, "God, we have had enough. No more violence. No more injustice. We want to see you bring healing and restoration to our communities. We want to see your people set free, no longer suffering under the dual oppressions of being a victim or being a perpetrator." I can imagine God saying to us, "As do I, my children. I grieve with you. Our hearts are broken together. I hate this violence. I despise this injustice. I am in agreement with you. I, too, want to bring healing and set people free. I am already working to change things. Continue to pray with me. Let's imagine how we can work creatively together to bring forth the vision of love we all want."

LISTENING WITH GOD

While praying with God, individuals and communities of faith are invited to practice listening *with* God. This prayerful and sacred tango involves mutual expression, listening to and feeling with one another. It also involves improvisation as both partners dialectically move off each other's steps. Samuel Williamson writes:

> Prayer is not a one-way street with us shouting petitions to God, and Scripture is not a one-way street of God broadcasting his commands at us. *Both* prayer and Scripture involve *both* hearing and speaking. We are participants, not spectators; dancers on the floor, not observers at the tables; actors on the stage, not onlookers in the theatre. We are involved in a divine dialogue.[4]

The dance between God and human beings is illustrated throughout the Bible. At first glance, it appears God spoke audibly with characters like Adam and Eve, Moses, Job, Jonah, Saul, Elijah, Peter, James, John, and Jesus. God speaking to them was not a *prompting, impression, impulse, nudge,* or *check.* God's communication with them was not veiled as an ambiguous two-word puzzle ("God gave me the words 'red' and 'Sarah'—um—at least I think he did"). Even God's famous "gentle whisper" to Elijah, which is used by Bible teachers as an example of what should be the norm of God speaking to Christians, was nevertheless in audible words and complete sentences (1 Kings 19).

Perhaps it is a semantic difference, but I suggest the phrase "God spoke *to* me" is a phrase that should be relegated more to the spectacular claims of the Bible. It describes a top-down, audible, external voice that comes to humans regardless of one's interest. God's speaking in an audible manner from the heavens (John 12:28), or from a cloud (Matthew 17:5; Mark 9:7), or through a bush, a donkey, or a prophet were miraculous exceptions to his normal pattern of speaking to a person from within. It is also possible that what was initially an inner *prompting* or *impression*, was, over time, mythologized into an audible voice by story-making and story-telling communities and, eventually, by creative biblical writers.

If we keep God's uncontrolling love in mind, it makes sense that God does not speak through a megaphone from heaven. God chooses to speak from within us rather than from outside of us. God speaks in collaboration with the hearer to avoid being controlling and coercive. Why? If God spoke in an externally audible way, he would have to force us to listen without an invitation and, therefore, without permission. Doing so would be a bit like if I were to break into the announcer's booth at a baseball game, grab a microphone, and tell the crowd about my political views. I would be acting in a coercive and controlling manner, forcing the crowd to listen to me without invitation or permission.

Some might present Saul in Acts as an example of God speaking audibly from the outside. A closer examination of the text reveals another possible interpretation. Saul saw a light from heaven flash around him, and he heard a voice say, "Saul, Saul, why do you persecute me?" (Acts 9:4). But the voice could well have come from within Saul. According to Acts 9:7, his fellow travelers heard a sound but they did not see anything. The sound could have been Saul being knocked off his horse and hitting the ground. We cannot be certain. According to Acts 22:9, however, his companions saw a light but did not hear anything. And in Acts 26:14, Saul is the only one who is reported to have heard anything verbal at all. The text is thus ambiguous, and it is possible that the voice Saul heard was one from within himself.

Whether the voice was audible or not, God was not intruding into Saul's life where he was not welcome. Saul was actually in regular prayer with God. He believed that persecuting the Christians, whom he saw as distorting the Jewish faith, was God's will. Saul had simply been unable to make the connection between the God to whom he prayed and Jesus. All along, Saul had been asking for God's guidance in his persecution of the church. Jesus's appearance to Saul was simply a dramatic moment within this prolonged conversation between Saul and God. Therefore, this story is not about God controlling or coercing Saul by speaking to him and forcing him to listen. Rather, Jesus simply asks him a question, and from there Saul opens the door to listen.

Some Christians suggest it is not that God *can't* communicate audibly, but that God chooses not to or that he does so only on very rare occasions. Leonard Sweet and Frank Viola write:

> Taking the whole of the New Testament together, it is our belief that when the Spirit spoke to someone in the book of Acts, it wasn't audible, but internal. We don't doubt that God may speak to some people audibly on rare occasion. But this isn't His normative way of speaking, either in Scripture or today.[5]

Although God, through the Holy Spirit, communicates to us all the time, he doesn't communicate *with* us without permission. The door of our heart needs to be open, even if only slightly. The *promptings, nudges,* and *impressions* should be reserved for these divine and human, naturally supernatural cooperative events. You will not find any New Testament writer saying, "God spoke to me." You will find phrases such as "led by the Spirit" (Matthew 4:1; Luke 4:1; Romans 8:14; Galatians 5:18), "moved by the Spirit" (Luke 2:27), "revealed by the Spirit" (Ephesians

3:5), "compelled by the Spirit" (Acts 20:22), or "guided" by the Spirit (John 16:13).

LISTENING FOR THE MISSION

We can learn from the New Testament writers and grow to recognize times when we feel led or compelled or moved by the Spirit. We can know the Spirit's leading will often pertain to God's mission, that is, what he wants us to do to expand his loving presence in the world. This was certainly the case for Jesus, who was on mission and had to continually commune and talk with God in order to know where to go and who to save, heal, and love. Jesus said, "The Son can do nothing by himself; he can do only what he sees his Father doing.... For the Father loves the Son and shows him all he does" (John 5:19–20). Jesus "saw" what the Father was doing by listening to him. Jesus surrendered to the presence of God. Jesus was completely reliant upon God, not only for the details of his mission but also for the power to complete it.

Mark 1:35, for example, says, "Very early in the morning, while it was still dark, Jesus got up, left the house and went off to a solitary place, where he prayed." Some of the disciples looked frantically for Jesus and eventually found him. By that time, Jesus had received his instructions and immediately told the group, "'Let us go somewhere else—to the nearby villages—so I can preach there also. That is why I have come.' So, he traveled throughout Galilee, preaching in their synagogues and driving out demons" (Mark 1:38–39). Jesus got away from the noise of those clamoring for his attention to spend time in intimacy with God. It was in that dark, solitary place that God told him where to go and what to do when he got there.

Job 33:14 says, "For God does speak—now one way, now another—though no one perceives it." God has no problem hearing when *we* talk. It is we who need to flex our spiritual antennas and practice receiving and actively listening to God's voice. Hearing God's voice, and listening to God's heartbeat for the world around us, is key in order for individuals and churches to achieve God's unique mission for the world.

It's not easy to make time to listen to God in our hustle-and-bustle culture. A lot of us have trouble sitting still for more than five minutes at a time, including myself. Silence and listening to God are foreign practices for many individuals and churches. God speaks all the time, yet we are way too busy with work, church, small groups, families, service projects, e-mails and texts, pop-up messages, social media, television shows, hobbies, and countless other things, to hear him.

Nevertheless, God invites us to create sacred spaces where we can be silent and practice the art of listening. A typical prayer meeting consists of people singing a few praise songs, stating their prayer requests, praying them to God, and returning home. There ought to be a time in that mix where the congregation turns down the guitar amps, shuts off the projector, zips their lips, quiets their hearts, and listens for what God might have to share. This old Quaker tradition is needed all the more in our high-tech age, regardless of denomination. When we can manage to shut out the noise, we can hear the loud whisper of God nudging us toward loving action and his kingdom vision of shalom.

THE ROYAL PRIESTHOOD

Participating in conspiring prayer and committing to engage in loving action in the world should not be done solely for the sake of "social justice." In other words, social justice does not need to be an end in itself. Granted, it is easy to do this in our current cultural milieu. Secular actors, musicians, and other celebrities give to charities, start non-profits, or become ambassadors of goodwill organizations. Our culture makes social justice sexy, and the church rides gleefully on its seductive coattails. While anyone who engages in social justice should be commended, I am suggesting that social justice should be done as a part of a grander story—God's story.

I suggest we engage in conspiring prayer for the sake of *God's* justice and kin(g)dom. It means joining our story within God's story. It means taking our calling as bearers of God's image and part of the chosen royal priesthood seriously. N. T. Wright brilliantly sums up our responsibility as those who profess the name of Christ. He writes:

> To reflect the divine image means standing between heaven and earth, even in the present time, adoring the Creator and bringing his purposes into reality on earth, ahead of the time when God completes the task and makes all things new. The "royal priesthood" is the company of rescued humans who, being part of "earth," worship the God of heaven and are thereby equipped, with the breath of heaven in their renewed lungs, to work for his kingdom on earth. The revolution of the cross sets us free to be in-between people, caught up in the rhythm of worship and mission.[6]

As priests, and divine echoes, we are called, then, to listen to and collaborate with God to passionately sync earth and heaven (Matthew 6:10). Such practice is not relegated to someone with a seminary degree. Listening, collaborating with God, and echoing the divine, is not just for the super-spiritual ones who claim God "speaks" to them audibly on a regular basis. We are *all* called to be on mission; that is, we are all called to follow a repeated pattern of prayer, silent listening, and collaborative action with the missionary God. Leonard Sweet reminds us, "God is a God of motion, of movement, of mission. Or, as it is popular nowadays to say, 'two-thirds of the word *God* is go.'"[7] We are called to pray with the intention to follow God's creative instructions, whatever they may be.

AN ATTITUDE OF GRATITUDE

Another element of conspiring prayer is praying with gratitude. Because God is not the author of evil and does not commit evil acts against others, we are aware even in the most terrible of circumstances that God can still be thanked. For example, the 9/11 attack was one of the worst tragedies in America's history. I was in New York at the time. I was vicariously traumatized watching the terrible events unfold. How could God be thanked in the midst of such a horrific event? Many people would say he shouldn't be, reasoning that God is in control and, therefore, that *God allowed it to happen.*

They are right in their logic. If God intentionally allowed 9/11 to occur, it would be hard to be thankful toward him. Saying God allowed 9/11 suggests that he could have disallowed it. In other words, saying "God allowed" suggests he could have stopped the evil event from happening. But this makes God out to be a voyeur who arbitrarily jumps into time, willfully intervening to stop some tragedies but not others. "God allows" suggests that through his inaction, God intentionally consents to each horrific or tragic event that occurs. Is that kind of understanding of how God works in the world a view we want to promote?

I propose we Christians get rid of the phrase "God allows." If we did, I suspect fewer people would be confused about God's role or, worse still, would blame God for the horrific events that occur. Eliminating "God allows" could remove an unnecessary cognitive and emotional obstacle that prevents many from having a loving and grateful connection with their Creator.

Those who find it difficult to thank an all-controlling and evil-permitting God in the aftermath of a tragedy have the right logic, but, unfortunately, they have a tainted view of God. God does not control and manipulate evil events according to his will. God hates evil and opposes it to his greatest capacity in light of human free will and other variables. Therefore, due to God's faithfulness and loving character, prayers of thanksgiving are deeply intertwined with conspiring prayers. Catholic theologian and social justice spokesman Henri Nouwen writes: "Every prayer of petition becomes a prayer of thanksgiving and praise as well, precisely because it is a prayer of hope. In the hopeful prayer of petition, we thank God for God's promise and we praise God for God's faithfulness."[8] Our hopeful prayers and petitions to God easily turn to thanksgiving and praise, especially as they marinate in the right view of a faithful and loving God. It is those kinds of prayers that will sustain us in the inevitability of tragic events and their aftermath.

Philippians 4:6 says, "Do not be anxious about anything, but in everything, by prayer and petition, with thanksgiving, present your requests to God." There would be no reason for Paul to write about the topic of anxiety if people weren't prone to feeling anxious. Certainly the Philippians had reasons to be anxious. They had real-life adversaries and the complexities of doctrinal soundness and sanctification to attend to. We are also prone to anxiety. Why wouldn't we be? It is easy to look at the news and wonder if tomorrow might be the demise of us all.

Regardless of the world we see around us, God's infinite, immanent, and active love and wisdom compel us to "give thanks in all circumstances" (1 Thessalonians 5:18). That is not to say God will change our circumstances. There are occasions when God does so with those who are willing to cooperate with him. There are other times when God simply can't. Paul doesn't give us false assurance that God will make our problems go away. However, Paul does say that when we talk to God, sharing our deepest anxieties with him, the peace of God that transcends all understanding will guard our hearts and our minds in Christ Jesus (Philippians 4:7).

God does not devise new, anxiety-provoking, or torturous ways to test and refine us. God continually loves all of creation toward shalom. Therefore, we aptly pray words of gratitude in the midst of conspiring prayers:

- "God, thank you for seeking to give wisdom to the doctors."

- "God, thank you for your desire to fill my dad with your love and peace."

- "God, thank you for seeking to end racism."

Of course, doctors may not be open to receiving God's wisdom. Dad may not be open to receiving God's love, healing, and peace. People might not be open to God's conviction and invitation to heal their pride, fear, and hate. Nonetheless, we can pray conspiring prayers in faith according to God's character and nature. We can rest assured that God does what God can do in each moment, and that is something to be grateful for.

CONSPIRING WITH GOD

A devastating avalanche enveloped a hotel in Italy on January 18, 2017, killing twenty-nine people and trapping nine more inside. As courageous rescuers made their way through the roof of the crushed structure, they heard the relieved survivors calling out, "Angels! Angels!"[9]

The word *angel* in the New Testament comes from the Greek word *angelos*, meaning simply *messenger*. These messengers can be celestial, such as Michael the archangel, or they can be human. In Matthew 11:10, John the Baptist is called an *angelos*. Those Italian heroes were rescuing angels—messengers of love and hope, not just in word but in action, too. They put their lives on the line for the sake of others. What would have happened if those rescuers hadn't heeded the call to come to the rescue of those in the hotel? I will tell you. Despite all the earnest prayers that would have been offered for them, at some point, most of them would have died.

Conspiring prayer involves life and death issues. The sacred practice helps us become angels who partner with God and listen to our mission; we take daring risks to be God's messengers of tangible hope and love in the world. In conspiring prayer, we don't talk *to* God in order to move him to increase his active love in the world. Instead, we partner *with* God in prayer; we hear his voice, align our will to his, and go out into the world as divine echoes advancing his empire of love.

David G. Benner is an internationally renowned psychologist, author, and spiritual teacher. He has written over two-dozen books. I read his transformational book *The Gift of Being Yourself* in a spiritual formation class for my seminary degree many years ago. In a blog, Benner details that after decades of praying in the traditional manner (to the one he now refers to as the "Cosmic Santa Claus who was prone to falling asleep"), he began to question the effectiveness of the practice.[10] It took many years, but eventually Benner began to "update" his understanding of prayer. He shares, "I didn't abandon my faith and

I didn't stop sharing my inner experience with God. But, I did abandon the cosmic Santa Claus who I had been taught could be moved into action on behalf of oneself or others by persistent knocking on the gates of heaven."[11]

If Benner no longer saw God as a "Cosmic Santa Claus," what did his updated view of prayer look like? Benner writes:

> I pray in order to give God transformational access to me, not for me to coerce God into doing me special favors. I do believe that God acts in the world in mysterious ways but now suspect that this is primarily through humans. Prayer slowly brings our self into alignment with God's self. This allows us to be attuned to and participate in God's healing, reconciling and transforming work in the world making all things more whole and more conscious of their existence in Christ.[12]

Mother Teresa eventually made the switch from traditional petitionary prayer to conspiring prayer. She is quoted as saying:

> I used to pray that God would feed the hungry, or do this or that, but now I pray that he will guide me to do whatever I'm supposed to do, what I can do. I used to pray for answers, but now I'm praying for strength. I used to believe that prayer changes things, but now I know that prayer changes us and we change things.[13]

Simply talking to God does not change the world. Prayerful people who commune deeply with God and engage the world around them change the world. Petitioning prayers that seek to woo God to love more actively will do nothing to alter the outcome for loved ones in need. Paul understood how necessary it was for the church to become the physical embodiment of the Spirit of God and to collaborate with a God who always desires salvation. He writes:

How, then, can they call on the one they have not believed in? And how can they believe in the one of whom they have not heard? And how can they hear without someone preaching to them? And how can anyone preach unless they are sent? As it is written: "How beautiful are the feet of those who bring good news!" (Romans 10:14–15)

For Paul, salvation requires a team effort. "How, then, can they call on the one they have not believed in?" The implication is, "They can't."

Paul says that God desires and needs human collaboration to accomplish his will. How can the rent be paid on your struggling friend's flat unless someone gives them money? How can racism be rooted out of the crevices of human hearts and minds unless someone teaches love and peace? How can child trafficking come to an end unless people stand up and rescue the children? How can environmental pollution be reduced unless individuals and corporations take practical steps? The answer to all of these questions is, "It can't."

Romans 10:15 says, "How beautiful are the feet of those who bring good news," not, "How beautiful are the words of those who bring good news." Unless people walk the walk and engage in Spirit-led and Spirit-empowered action, then salvation, justice, and shalom will not become realities in the world we live in.

Jason, whose mother Debby, you'll recall, prays for his salvation, needs a prayerful person filled with God's love to preach the good news to him in word and deed. This paradigm shift moves us from petitionary prayers such as, "God, pour out your love on Jason," or, "God, save Jason," to, "God, thank you for your love and mercy. Thank you for your love for Jason and your steadfast desire to save him. We both long for you to pour out your love on him. Show us, as your hands and feet, how to practically plant seeds of love in Jason's life and how to water them so you can make them grow and Jason can be saved" (see 1 Corinthians 3:6).

Teresa of Ávila, a sixteenth-century nun and mystic, had a profound revelation of the church being the literal hands and feet of God on the earth. She writes:

Christ has no body now but yours,

No hands, no feet on earth but yours,

Yours are the eyes through which he looks compassion on this world,

Yours are the feet with which he walks to do good,

Yours are the hands through which he blesses all the world.

Yours are the hands, yours are the feet,

Yours are the eyes, you are his body.

Christ has no body now on earth but yours.[14]

CONCLUSION

The sovereignty of God, when misunderstood by Christians as "God is in control of everything," is one of the most detrimental, devilish doctrines and deterrents to human flourishing that I know. I realize the doctrine attempts to portray God as powerful above all else, including the most destructive circumstances, thereby enhancing his praiseworthiness. It is thus an attempt to prop God up, which is a semi-noble endeavor. Nevertheless, the cost is too high.

This "God-is-in-control-of-everything" theology lulls Christians into becoming passive observers and siren-induced sleepwalkers. It can potentially cause people to lackadaisically go about their life and throw up an occasional prayer because, ultimately, "God is in control." Meanwhile, greed, oppression,

*good for nothing
or
good for something!*

poverty, sexual violence, murder, genocide, and other systemic injustices increase. It is theology gone wrong.

Christians who remain stagnant because of inaccurate theology are doing the world no good. If Christians use the "God-is-in-control-of-everything" card to cover up their existential anxiety in the midst of devastating events or as a way to avoid getting their hands dirty in a messy world, the results can be harmful and destructive. Sometimes sins of omission are just as harmful as sins of commission. Therefore, we are in need of heartbroken, holy-discontented, kingdom-minded people who hear and heed the call to radically bring love to the world by becoming the active hands and feet of God.

Conspiring prayer has nothing to do with a secular humanistic agenda. I am not encouraging Christians, apart from God, to pick themselves up by their bootstraps and use their superior intellect and resources to save the world. I am seeking fully surrendered God-lovers who listen *with* God in humility, hear God speak within the depths of their souls, and allow God to empower them toward active engagement in the world. Shane Claiborne says it well: "We need to pray like everything depends on God and live like God has no other plan but the church."[15] The most transformative prayers are not those by which we attempt to change God, but those in which we open ourselves up to God as the body of Christ. Through them, God can change and transform us so we can become "imitators of God" (Ephesians 5:1) and work for the transformation of the world around us.

So often, we cry out to God to move mightily in our loved ones' lives or to move mightily in the midst of catastrophe, and we ask, "God, where are you?"

Ironically, God is asking, "Where are *you*?"

The answers to our prayers for friends, neighbors, loved ones, and nations are not found in a movement of God alone. They

*eg * Peter dozing on the roof + having a vision of food → goup to Cornelius's house!*

are found in God moving in and through us as his hands and feet. Will we answer the call?

In the next chapter, we will explore the practical application of prayer through case studies with a view of God's uncontrolling love in mind.

CHAPTER 9

CONSPIRING PRAYER
IN ACTION

We have investigated and deconstructed petitionary prayer on behalf of others. We have also reconstructed petitionary prayer by exploring the biblical, theological, and philosophical principles of conspiring prayer. This concluding chapter will explore conspiring prayer through real-life case studies. All theological certainties must become experiential and liberating realities. Theology must be practically lived out and loved out.

Conspiring prayer is not marked with God's golden seal of approval, deemed pre-eminent above all others. It is by no means the definitive approach. It is one of many effective forms of petitionary prayer. What makes it novel and paradigm-shifting is how it integrates God's uncontrolling, loving nature in a framework that incorporates a compelling theodicy with a viable and transformational praxis.

Some individuals and churches may already be practicing conspiring prayer without realizing it. After reading this book, they may continue to pray as they always have yet feel the need to tweak their theology. For them, it is not reimagining prayer but rather reorienting themselves while praying in a way that they have always considered invaluable. Others may tweak both their prayer practice and the theology behind it in subtle ways while still others might take conspiring prayer and morph it into something that better fits their unique community.

In the first case study, I examine Tony Campolo's prayer at the 2016 Democratic National Convention through the lens of conspiring prayer. Next, I discuss a hypothetical church engaging in conspiring prayer for a congregation member recovering in a hospital after a car accident. After this, I view a brave woman's engagement with both God and the deadly streets of Chicago. Finally, I present conspiring prayers that can be offered in light of the tragedies of mass shootings and mental illness.

THE 2016 DEMOCRATIC NATIONAL CONVENTION

Tony Campolo, a well-known Christian pastor, author, sociologist, and social activist, prayed a petitionary prayer at the 2016 Democratic National Convention. Looking at his heartfelt invocation through the lens of conspiring prayer, I can see a few areas of fine-tuning that I would consider to make his prayer more effective in promoting shalom. Here are the opening lines:

> Dear God, we are a nation that needs healing. Break down the barriers of race and ethnicity that separate us. Cure the sexism and homophobia that deny the dignity of so many of our fellow Americans. Show us how to love the needy in our midst—and even our enemies. Help us overcome evil with good.

A traditional understanding of petitionary prayer places the responsibility on God to bring about love, healing, and grace to those who are prayed for, while conspiring prayer places the responsibility on both God and the petitioner. Conspiring prayer also keeps in mind God's uncontrolling, loving character and individual free will.

Campolo's first line, "Dear God, we are a nation that needs healing," fits within the model of conspiring prayer. While God knows that the nation needs healing and grieves with us, sharing the pangs of grief with God about the injustice we see in the world is a beautiful and relational act.

The remedy that Campolo alludes to in the second and third lines is only halfway correct. It is not God alone who needs to "break down barriers of race and ethnicity" or "cure the sexism and homophobia." These problems require our participation.

Unfortunately (or fortunately, depending on how you look at it), God is not in control. If God had his way, the barriers of race and ethnicity would have been broken down a long time ago. In God "there is neither Jew nor Gentile, neither slave nor free, nor is there male and female, for you are all one in Christ Jesus" (Galatians 3:28). God is much more interested in the heart than in the outward appearance and the labels we place on one another (1 Samuel 16:7). Our partnering with God will break down the barriers of race and ethnicity so that we can experience unity amidst diversity. Praying to God for basic needs such as ridding our country of sexism and homophobia and expecting God to unilaterally accomplish the request is immature. Immature is not bad. It is not like God grades our prayers. But we are after mature and effective prayer.

Campolo's prayer would have been more in the spirit of conspiring prayer had he been specific and honest about where the barriers of sexism and homophobia were located and asked God to remove them. The barriers of racism, homophobia, and sexism reside in the hearts of the people who were in that very room. Therefore, to pray, "Break down the barriers of race and ethnicity in *our* hearts," and, "Cure the sexism and homophobia in *our* hearts," would be more effective.

Petitionary prayers that hope God will unilaterally root out societal ills and heal our nation of 'isms' are magical and superstitious. God has an open-door policy. God can't root out racism, sexism, and homophobia in hearts that refuse to let him in. We must take seriously our role as free agents in the world. "You do it, God" types of prayers will never be as transformative as "How can we do it, God?" types of prayers. That is why it is best to ask God for the grace to repent and the power to heal and love the other unconditionally. Adding "our" to Campolo's prayers is not just semantics. Little shifts in the way we pray can make a considerable difference over time.

Remember, because of his loving nature, God cannot single-handedly control the will of human beings. Or, if people prefer, God, for the most part, chooses not to single-handedly control and forcefully intervene in the lives of others. American philosopher William Hasker takes the "can, but chooses not to" approach. He writes:

> Frequent and routine intervention by God to prevent the misuse of freedom by his creatures and/or to repair the harm done by this misuse would undermine the structure of human life and community intended in the plan of creation; accordingly, such intervention should not be expected to occur.[1]

Whatever view a person holds on whether God can or cannot control others, God usually does nothing in or through people without their cooperation. Therefore, Campolo's last two requests are congruent with conspiring prayer and God's uncontrolling nature: "Show us how to love the needy in our midst—and even our enemies. Help us overcome evil with good." The key words are "show us" and "help us." To pray, "God, show us," is far more potent than, "God, show them."

"Show us" types of prayers will be more effective in making our corporate petitions a reality. God's ability to root out racism correlates with our ability to open the doors of our hearts in surrender to God's love and in obedience to God's loving principles.

One last opportunity for effectiveness in line with conspiring prayer is to stop and listen after the "show us" request has been made. To ask God to "show us" and then not allow God to fulfill that request is an empty prayer. While God knows the heart of the one who prays and its sincerity, God also needs access to the heart to speak his message and share his mission. Obviously, Campolo had a limited amount of time for his prayer. The Democratic National Convention was not a church service. Nevertheless, the prayer would have been more effective if he had led the attendees in a moment of silence.

Silence is one of the most effective acts a person can engage in to rid the heart of idolatry. Silence gives God an opportunity to expose the shadows within. It creates a moment for God to break open new pathways for his light to shine in the world and for petitioners to creatively imagine how they can love the needy and their enemies in the future.

CONSPIRING PRAYERS FOR SARAH

Another example of my proposed paradigm shift to conspiring prayer is a local church's prayers for Sarah. Sarah, a member of the church, was involved in a car accident on a Monday and went to hospital as a result of her injuries. She was to have surgery in a few days. Church members met on Wednesday evening and engaged in conspiring prayer.

God loved that the church came together in unity to pray for Sarah. They were a congregation that took tremendous pride in carrying each other's burdens and fulfilling the loving law of Christ (Galatians 6:2). God valued their relationship and loved that they talked with him. "The righteous cry out, and the LORD hears them" (Psalm 34:17). God entered into the depths of their souls, from which their words flowed, and heard every word. If all the church did was stand together in solidarity and share their desires for Sarah, God would consider it a beautiful act.

The church's theology and theodicy, which prioritizes God's uncontrolling love, informed their practice of petitionary prayer. The church leaders trained and equipped the church in the conspiring model. Therefore, they believed that God loves to his greatest ability in every moment while respecting free will and other agencies in the process. They took pleasure in God's immanence and relational nature. They embraced the revelation of God's wonderful presence with them even before they went into the sanctuary to pray.

The church understood that praying petitionary prayers as a means to move God unilaterally to increase his active love in Sarah's life, especially for her basic needs of healing and wholeness, would have little effect. The church shared their heart with God even though they did not believe God could magically defy lawlike regularities and unilaterally control the outcome. That belief did not cause them anxiety. They did what was natural regardless of the outcome, which was to be relational. Theologian and civil rights leader Howard Thurman writes:

> When the hunger for God becomes articulate in a man so that it is one with his initial experience of God, it is the most natural thing in the world to share whatever his concerns may be. A man prays for loved ones because he has to, not

merely because his prayer may accomplish something beyond this.[2]

The church embraced God's care for them and naturally shared their concerns with him. They had an abiding faith and trust that God was doing everything possible to help Sarah. The church not only shared their deepest desire for Sarah, they prayed prayers of faith and thanksgiving in line with God's loving nature. One member spoke out loud, "Thank you, God, for being the first on the scene of the accident. Nothing is hidden from your sight."

The church also knew God's heart was grieved because Sarah was hurting and in need of medical care. They prayed, "Thank you for caring for Sarah. We grieve with you, knowing she is your daughter and our sister."

Even though they knew God was actively loving to the extent that God could, someone still said, "God, we pray that you would give the doctors wisdom in caring for Sarah and that the doctors would receive it." They did not pray petitions to move God to intervene unilaterally and instantly inject the doctors with wisdom whether the doctors wanted it or not. Rather, they simply prayed in order to share their heart and their wishes with God. They knew that God loves his children to cast their cares upon him because he cares for them (1 Peter 5:7). They prayed what they believed in accordance with God's will and with a mutual vision of loving care for Sarah. They also prayed, "God, thank you for healing Sarah right now and thank you for seeking to comfort the family. May they embrace your love in this moment of grief and uncertainty." Each prayer, hope, wish, and longing corresponded with God's loving and uncontrolling nature.

The church began to pray beautifully dangerous partnering prayers. They were *dangerous* in the sense that the prayers required courage and risk. They prayed, "God we want to join you in what you are already doing for Sarah. Show us how to love her. Show us how to be your hands and feet."

The church members began to be silent with God. They allowed the Holy Spirit to speak to them. They fully embraced what was once uncomfortable in their Christian walk because silence is the medium of the wonders of God. It is a place where "deep calls to deep" (Psalm 42:7) and the sacred mission can be received.

After a few minutes of silence, the pastor spoke and asked the members, "Did anyone hear anything specific while listening with God?" Nancy, a beloved friend of Sarah since they were kids, raised her hand. "I am not sure whether it is God, or me, or both of us, but I feel a strong sense that I should briefly meet with the doctors before her surgery. I am going to be at the hospital with her husband for her surgery anyway. I want to ask if I could pray with them. I am grateful to know they have already received God's wisdom and training in becoming a doctor. My hope is that they would be open to receive God's wisdom and sharpness of mind just prior to the surgery." Since a thousand people per day die from preventable errors in hospitals, Nancy's request was prudent.[3]

Nancy knew that praying in solidarity with God for the doctors, which is where traditional petitionary prayer usually stops, was only the first step. She knew that partnering with God in action was the next step. And she understood that the doctors needed to be open to receive God's additional wisdom for Sarah's unique situation. What better way to be a catalyst for that opening than to visit and pray with them? Nancy took a risk. She could easily be rejected, but such is the daring adventure of the Christian life.

The church prayed other partnering prayers during their gathering. Many members heard a specific battle plan for what they called "Operation Loving Sarah." A few of the members listened with God and decided to form a meal train to make sure Sarah's husband, who was not a believer, and their two children ate well during Sarah's recovery. Other members taught Sunday School and felt a nudge to get the children involved by drawing encouraging cards for Sarah. More specific and practical ideas of how to love Sarah and her family materialized as the meeting went on. The church members partnered with God in petitionary prayer. They felt energized in their faith and were excited for what God was doing in and through them. Sarah recovered well and her family was loved and supported because of an incredible God and a prayerful community,

Are you starting to notice the difference between Petitionary Prayer 1.0 and Petitionary Prayer 2.0 (conspiring prayer)? I hope you can see the exciting potential conspiring prayer holds for congregations. In a traditional prayer meeting, the congregation could have easily said a few sincere prayers, hoping they would influence God to increase his loving activity in Sarah's life, and called it a night. There is much good in those prayers, but with these few tweaks in understanding and practice, I hope you can see they can be even more effective and impactful.

CONSPIRING PRAYER IN CHICAGO

Gang violence is a serious problem in the United States. Every day, senseless shootings tear apart families, inspire vengeance, and perpetuate the cycle of violence. Chicago is one of the cities where gang violence has become an epidemic. For many, the streets of Chicago feel unsafe. As I write over the Christmas weekend in 2016, at least twenty-seven people have been shot, and at least seven have died.[4] Petitionary prayers asking God alone to reduce gun violence and transform the city will not be enough. It will take those who engage God in conspiring prayer to start making a dent in this tragic issue.

Tamar Manasseh, a student of Judaism and lover of God, didn't want to merely talk about doing something in her hometown of Chicago, so she decided to partner with God in prayer and do something about the violence. Howard Thurman believed petitionary prayers for others allow one to be open to another person's plight and expose their need to one's "total life and resources, making it possible for new insights of helpfulness and creativity to emerge."[5] It was through prayer that Tamar found new creative insights to help members in her community. In a private correspondence with me, she wrote:

> I never know what's going to happen day to day. There are really no plans. It just seems that when I awaken each morning, I have a set of instructions for the day which I carry out. I may have my own ideas [about] how things may turn out or even my own personal hopes for what I wish the outcome to be. However, ultimately, I know nothing and decide nothing. I just wait until the ending or the next move is revealed to me. I strongly believe that God reveals to us all our purpose and our role in "tikkun olam," repairing the world. However, it is up to each of us whether or not we will ... accept the job.[6]

Tamar shared her heart's cry for justice with God, listened to God in prayer, heard his creative instruction, and obeyed. She formed Mothers Against Senseless Killings, or MASK.[7] She decided to go out to one of the street corners plagued with rampant violence and enact the love of God through loving presence. She also recruited "an army of moms" to do the same. They shared stories, gave out food, and connected with people in the community. Because of her partnering-prayer with God, there has not been another shooting on that corner.[8] Granted, the problem of gun violence has not subsided in Chicago. In some parts, violence has become worse. However, at least for the time being, that war-torn corner knows shalom. Shalom came because someone engaged in conspiring prayer, listened for instruction, and took enormous risks to become a divine echo of God.

CONSPIRING PRAYERS AND MASS SHOOTINGS

Mass shootings are becoming too common. For many of us, the names of Pulse nightclub, Virginia Tech, Las Vegas, and Sandy Hook Elementary take us back to the initial terror and fear we felt when we first heard the news. They remind us of the helplessness and sadness we experienced for the victims and their loved ones and of our gut-wrenching cry and lament to God.

How do we pray for mass shootings from a perspective of conspiring prayer? First, let me share some traditional petitionary prayers that are often prayed after such incidents:

- "I pray for the victims, families, and first responders."
- "God, be with the families of those shooting victims."
- "Pour out your grace on the surviving family members."
- "Comfort and heal their wounded hearts."
- "Rid the nation of violence."
- "Turn from your fierce anger; relent and do not bring further disaster on your people." (Exodus 32:12)

What beautiful-sounding prayers! (Well, perhaps the last one could use a little adjustment.) They come from passionate, well-meaning people of faith. But while they are meaningful in one sense, are they really in line with the character of God's uncontrolling love? Do they make sense within the framework of a coherent theodicy? Do they make a good God look bad? Do they take into consideration other agencies, such as free will or the laws of nature?

Let's look at the first stand-alone prayer: "I pray for the victims, families, and first responders." It is very common for people to say, "I pray," and then mention the person or circumstance and leave it at that. But saying the words "I pray" doesn't mean anything. The phrase has no magical power. I used to pray like that, too. "Dear Heavenly Father, I pray for my dad and my brother." "I pray for my school test tomorrow." "I pray for all the hurting victims of that heinous crime." Although God is gracious enough to look at the heart and can consider such prayers, there are more effective ways to pray.

Let's look at the prayers, "God, be with the families of those shooting victims," "Pour out your grace on the surviving family members," and, "Comfort and heal their wounded hearts." Those who use the conspiring prayer model already know God is with those families. They trust that God, in his loving character, comforts and heals wounded hearts to the degree he is able while respecting their free will. God grieves along with the devastated families. God's grace has been poured out in their lives and is instantly available to them in even greater measure if they choose to open the doors of their hearts to him.

We can share our desires for hurting loved ones with God to experience more of his presence, grace, and comfort, knowing full well God wants them to experience more of those things too. Or we can pray without trusting in the goodness of God, thinking that in order for them to experience more of his presence, grace, and comfort, we need to pray fervently and convince God to provide more of those things.

Now, we will turn to the prayers, "God rid the nation of violence," and, "Turn from your fierce anger; relent and do not bring further disaster on your people." First, we have no need to convince God to rid the nation of violence. God hates violence. The psalmist says, "The Lord examines the righteous, but the wicked, those who love violence, he hates with a passion" (Psalm 11:5 NLT). Although I think the psalmist was a little over the top and I don't think God hates the *person*, I do think God hates violence with a passion. Violence is sin, and sin ruptures, fractures, wounds, distorts, and numbs our relationship with God, with ourselves, and with others.

Second, God does everything he can to rid the world of violence, but his uncontrolling love keeps him from intervening in every instance of violence. The people who do not listen to God or obey God's loving directives are responsible for the violence that we see. Mass shootings were committed by people who said, "No!" to God's whispers to love, honor, and protect.

Third, the writer of Exodus who penned, "Relent and do not bring further disaster on your people," had an inaccurate portrait of God. He assumed that it was God who brings "disaster" and violence upon people. If we took the writer's portrayal of God and put it through the lens of the Quadrilateral Hermeneutic of Love, we could conjecture that that writer was culturally conditioned. His version of God, like many versions of God in his time period, consisted of a God who used violence to punish sin. Love is kind and seeks to protect. Love does not commit violence.

The current doomsday preachers and angry prophetic teachers who look at violence, especially on a mass scale, and say that it is due to God's will, need to hang out with Jesus more often. It is one thing to pray like Habakkuk—"How long, Lord, must I call for help, but you do not listen? Or cry out to you, 'Violence!' but you do not save?" (Habakkuk 1:2)—because we don't understand where God is in the midst of our suffering. It is another to blame God for that suffering. The world in which we live is a world where God is not in control and where people have free will. A loving God would not coerce someone, let alone coerce them to shoot others.

Here is a prayer that can be offered after a mass shooting that keeps in mind God's uncontrolling, loving character and human free will:

God, we praise you for being good. Thank you for being intimately close to the families of the victims of this horrific shooting. We know you are grieved and mourn with us. We are aware you are angry that this has happened again. Heavenly, Earthly, Motherly Father, we need this violence to stop, now. It tears our communities and this world apart. It breaks our hearts and we know it breaks yours. We thank you that you comfort and mend the families' broken hearts to the extent that you are able. We hope that the families accept your love and experience your tenderness toward them in this painful time. Faithful God, what can we do together to stop this madness, or, at the very least, to help these families experience your tangible love? We don't want to be passive bystanders. We want to be Spirit-led, active adventurers, paving the way for justice, peace, and healing. God, we attune our hearts' ears to your voice at this moment. What is it that you would have us do as your hands and your feet so that your empire of love can reign in this hour? Amen.

PETITIONARY PRAYER AND MENTAL ILLNESS

Mental illness is cruel. What it has done to my brother's life is downright evil. It is a condition that God had no part in desiring, creating, or sustaining. There are other dynamics I keep in mind when I think about the origin of my brother's condition. Mental illness has been in my family for generations (nature). Generational patterns of dysfunctional and abusive ways of relating have contributed to my brother's condition (nurture). Of course, societal and individual moral choices have contributed to my brother's fate as well. Despite all these factors, I know God has always sought to heal, restore, and deliver my brother to freedom.

Holding to a theodicy that understands God not to be a cruel scriptwriter who intentionally gave my brother mental illness has changed the way I pray. I don't have to hold back cognitive dissonance and its byproduct of distrust toward God. I don't have to be confused. I don't need to constantly push down my anger due to believing in a God who supposedly loves my brother and can heal him in an instant but refuses to do so for some odd but well-meaning purpose. Let me share a conspiring prayer that I have prayed for my brother:

God, I am sick to my stomach. I can't imagine what my brother goes through in that desolate cell. The prison system is a mess. He's all alone, without care, without comfort, and without family and the familiarity of safe and accepting people. God, thank you for your love for him. I know you know what it is like to suffer and to feel abandoned. You have felt the sting of rejection and the madness of being tormented by your accusers all the way to your last breath. I know our hearts mutually ache for him, but aching is not enough. I long for you to save him and make his mind whole. I long for you to set him free. I want him to be in his right mind and to have normal conversations without paranoia and anger. I know you desire him to experience those as well. God, I take this time to listen to your voice. I pray for your wisdom and for creativity to know how to co-labor with you and love my brother and your precious son more effectively. Amen.

Do I wish God would instantly heal my brother? Absolutely! But although God desires to heal my brother, his powerful love is not compulsory. God cannot force my brother's faulty neurons to fire properly. God cannot be a divine therapist who instantaneously heals my brother's ravaged psyche, particularly without any cooperation from my brother. God can't compel my brother to accept his help. Peter Baelz, who was a former professor of moral and pastoral theology at Oxford, writes:

> Love requires freedom. It makes no sense to think that love can compel or manipulate a loving response. In giving freedom, love has to let go...There are, then, many things which sheer power can do but which boundless love cannot do.[9]

God's power is paradoxically uncontrolling, loving power. Paul says that the "weakness of God is stronger than human strength" (1 Corinthians 1:25). As powerful as God's boundless love is, it appears weak because God invites cooperation to accomplish his purposes. But God's empowering and healing presence, which always non-coercively woos and invites us toward shalom, is stronger than the forceful, controlling, manipulating, and narcissistic love of human beings. It is true that God's loving and weak power can get the job done much more slowly than more forceful and coercive approaches, but it is the only power able to sustain lasting and liberating change.

For my brother, I can pray thanking God for who God is and what he has done, is doing, and will do in the future. I can view God with loving assurance, knowing he is not withholding healing for my brother on purpose. In other words, it is not that God can heal my brother but chooses not to, and especially not because I have not earned it by praying or fasting enough. It is that God cannot override the will of my brother, nor forcefully manipulate other variables that might be keeping him sick and diseased. God is good all the time. Unfortunately, not every variable is open to God's goodness.

One such variable that God cannot instantaneously change is the inadequate prison system, which is not conducive to the healing of mentally ill patients. I am convinced that it is certainly an obstacle to my brother's recovery. For example, it is not God who forces my brother to live in sub-par conditions. God didn't leave him in isolation for months at a time. God doesn't refuse him phone-calls to people who love him and who can encourage him. God doesn't force him to eat food devoid of proper nutrition. God doesn't ridicule him and mock him. It is the prison system and the guards who treat my brother poorly and rob him of the necessary ingredients for a right mind and a healed heart. Does God want to change the system? Absolutely! But God can do nothing to the system without us, his hands and feet. It will take people who open the doors of their hearts to the God of love and justice to change it.

I do hold a future hope for my brother. While I have hopes and dreams for him in this life, I hope that one day the fire of God's luminous love will burn away all the seeds of evil that have affected and infected us. It is my hope that messy relationships, heartbreak, mental illness, poverty, and racism will be things of the past.

In Revelation 21:4, John records a profound glimpse of the moment when heaven and earth will be restored and all will be made whole: "He will wipe every tear from their eyes. There will be no more death or mourning or crying or pain, for the old order of things has passed away." A day will come when God will gently wipe away the troublesome tears from our weary eyes with his strong and tender healing hand. Death will be no more. There will also be no more loss, no more pain, and no more mental illness.

In that future hope, we will finally be able to love one another without our egos or trauma getting in the way. Faith will replace fear, love will replace hate, purity will replace manipulation, and goodness will replace evil. We will experience the purest intimate relationships with God and others, filled with love, affection, and community. One day, we will enjoy a perfect and new kind of love in a place where disease and dis-ease will be no more. Until then, we prayerfully partner with God, echo his love, and slowly collide heaven and earth.

CONCLUSION

Conspiring prayer is a reimagined prayer paradigm that avoids placing all the responsibility on God and instead seeks to actively join God in becoming a blessing to the world. Author and theologian Marjorie Suchocki beautifully writes:

> Through prayer we open ourselves to the divine will so that the guidance fashioned for us in heaven might be felt and effected on earth. We change the world by molding the world toward the divine concern for well-being in justice, renewal of nature, and openness and peace among all peoples.[10]

We need now more than ever to engage in embodied conspiring prayers. Paul writes, "Be imitators of God, as beloved children, and live in love, as Christ loved us and gave himself up for us" (Ephesians 5:1–2a NRSV). We are called to silence our busy lives, seek God in prayer, hear his heartbeat, perform the unique mission he has for us, and echo his non-coercive, uncontrolling love in the world.

Over the past few months, I have been outraged at the situation in Syria, at towns decimated, families broken, and innocent people killed. The horrific images of war-torn children staring back at me with their sullen eyes and postures of fear have brought me to tears. I can't help but think how many people might be saved (in the broad and holistic sense of the word) if we prayed conspiring prayers instead of traditional petitionary prayers.

I wonder what the impact would be if, instead of praying, "God, stop the violence," "God, heal their land," or "God, save the poor children," our first impulse was to pray, "God, we praise you, we thank you, and we know you care more about these people than we do. Show us how we can collaborate with you to stop the violence. Show us impactful and practical ways we can partner with you and heal their land. God, we are devastated along with you; reveal to us your loving will and empower us to bring forth shalom for these hurting children."

Can you imagine what kind of world we would live in if God-lovers did not falsely believe God was in control of all things? Can you imagine the wondrous extent of God's rule of love and shalom on the earth if we took the idea of stewardship and our identity as the body of Christ on the earth seriously? Can you imagine all the people who would be saved, restored, healed, loved, rescued, empowered, and showered with grace if superstitious praying—believing an all-powerful, autocratic God will miraculously intervene all by himself—did not get in the way of responsible, Spirit-filled action?

I cannot help but wonder if my mother would be alive today and my brother would not be walking as the living dead if people, including myself, embraced conspiring prayer. What would have happened if Christians who interacted with my mom and brother didn't believe God was in control but embraced God's uncontrolling love, felt the weight and sense of urgency to be the hands and feet of God in their lives, and knelt at the feet of Jesus, to listen for instructions? I realize we have no guarantees. No matter how much love was extended to them through God's body, they could still have chosen to say yes or no to that love. But an increased probability for shalom always exists when love-filled, prayerful people engage the world around them.

Nothing would be lost if we updated our petitionary prayer operating system. We only have transformation and liberation to gain. The time and energy spent praying to God and believing that he will take care of it all by himself could be used to mobilize people of faith to take risks and love practically. Petitionary prayer for others cannot be an opiate lulling us to lazy living. We must no longer give in to its delusions that become obstacles to what God longs to accomplish in the world. We can no longer behold human subjugation, oppression, and atrocities believing, "God is in control and he will take care of it in his time." Once we realize God does not solve our problems alone, we can drench ourselves in God's love as individuals and communities, dive heart-first into the world's blistering traumas, and expand God's empire of shalom across the earth.

I would say that change is in order, but "change" is too small a word. What we need is a revolution. As the great Protestant theologian Karl Barth observed, "To clasp the hands in prayer is the beginning of an uprising against the disorder of the world."[11]

The topsy-turvy force of love, led by the Spirit as Captain with a trajectory of justice, knocks on the doors of our hearts and waits for us to open up, receive our subversive instruction, and engage in our individual and communal mission.

Change alone is difficult, never mind a full-on revolution! Some churches will have a difficult time shifting from one paradigm to another. Conspiring prayers involve having courage and taking risks. It is easier to pray and let God handle it than to pray and collaborate with God. The anxious voices crying, "But this is the way we have always done it," will be plentiful. Yet too much is on the line. Systemic injustices of all kinds ravage people and creation. The world cries out unawares for gospel-filled, prayed-up, kingdom-minded warriors of love. The church should be the salt of the earth and moonlight to the world, reflecting the love and light of the Son in both word and deed.

A paradigm shift regarding petitionary prayer for others is in order. A powerfully loving God doesn't need to be reminded or talked into doing what is intrinsic to his nature. It is we, the church, who are called now more than ever to "act justly and to love mercy and to walk humbly with" our God (Micah 6:8). Let us pray more effective and less harmful prayers. Let us avoid praying in a way that makes God look bad, not only for God's sake but for the sake of the world. Let us become divine echoes!

COMMUNAL PRAYERS

The following communal prayers by various authors, scholars, and laypersons are examples of "conspiring prayer" and are grounded in God's uncontrolling love, issues of social justice, and human partnership.

OPENING SERVICE PRAYER[1]

Gracious and Loving God,
you love it when we come together to be with you.
We thank you for a new day and another opportunity
to meet together to worship and acknowledge you.
We honor and welcome your presence today;
open our eyes to all you want to do among
us by your life-giving Spirit.
Help us to be expectant and to leave knowing that
today we have met with the Risen Christ.
Help us to know in life-transforming ways
of the vast extent of your passionate love for us
and of your forgiveness and grace.
Help us to know in our heads and hearts that you are truly with us
in all our complex life circumstances.
Help us now to relax in your presence and receive
the good things you want to give us.
Give us the freedom to worship you wholeheartedly,
our Maker, Redeemer, and Sustainer.
We ask this with the authority of your son
Jesus, the Messiah and our Savior.
Amen.

OPENING PRAYER FOR UNITY AND MINDFULNESS[2]

God of Blessing,
you call all creation to new and abundant life.
By your Spirit, the earth and all living things flourish—
plants and trees, birds, beasts,
insects, reptiles, fish, people, and every other living organism.
We pray for
the well-being of all your creation,
understanding of our diversity and difference,
peace in our communities, with our neighbors,
and with those of different faiths,
hope and healing for indigenous peoples,
and reconciliation in the wider community.
Keep us mindful of the mistakes of the past,
and help us not to repeat them.
Amen.

BENEDICTION FOR WANDERERS[3]

Now, as you go,
wandering in dusty circles
through wilderness, longing for the Promised Land,
know that God wanders with you,
reveling in each step,
full of delight at the time spent with you.
So, wander!
Wander and be fruitful,
wander and grow,
wander and receive your new name—
Beloved.
Wander and know
that you do not wander alone.
Wander in Peace.
Amen.

PRAYER FOR THE HOMELESS AND THEIR LOVED ONES[4]

Dear God, we lift up to you those who
are homeless this evening.
We also pray for those who love them, who
may be feeling helpless to aide them.
You already know all of the wonderful
possibilities for good in this situation.
We know that you are always working
for their continuous well-being.
Open our eyes to ways we can be of assistance
to these individuals and their families.

*(Let us take a moment of silence and listen with
God for how we may creatively love them)*

May their hearts be open to cooperate with your Spirit
in making wise choices, remaining safe, and discerning
the good possibilities from the bad as they arise.
Also, uphold their families during the uncertain
times they find themselves in.
Whether it is unknown where a loved one is
tonight or whether that loved one is OK,
may they reach out and commune with
you, the God of all comfort
and the God who never leaves or forsakes them.
May their communion with you give them
peace and soothe their anxious hearts.
In the name of Jesus, thank you for hope.
Amen.

THESE HANDS: A PRAYER[5]

(People stand, hands over chest.)

We take a few deep breaths.

*(Pause for at least three breaths. Then make
fists and raise them line by line.)*

We live in a time of clenching fists:
in anger that threatens,
in greed that clutches,
in worry and fear that tense and tighten.
This is no way to live.

(Open hands and thrust them outward, as if breaking chains.)

And so, we let go.
We take a few deep breaths.

*(Pause. Lower hands, palms open, facing
upward, raising them line by line.)*

Our hands are empty.
We acknowledge our powerlessness.
We are not in control.
We are but humble protagonists in your great story of love.
We receive your grace that heals, forgives, and liberates.
This is the way to live.
And so, we open our hands, our hearts, our minds, our doors.
Ahhhh!

We take a few deep breaths.

(Facing palms outward, raise them line by line.)

We extend our hands in blessing.
As we have been blessed, so we bless.
We hold no weapons and make no threats.
We seek peace with all and we make peace for all.
It is better for us to give than to receive.
Make us instruments of your peace, Living God.
We surrender our lives to your purposes.
May your Spirit fill our lives and work through these hands.
Amen!
We take a few deep breaths.

(Pause, hands pressed together over heart)

We open our eyes.
We see your light in one another:
a flickering candle in the dark,
a quiet glow at dawn,
a rising sun for this new day.
We call forth that light in one another,
and we honor one another with these hands.
May the peace of Christ rise in you.

(People silently turn and honor one another,
praying a silent blessing over each other.)

PRAYER TO THE ONE WHO IS LOVE[6]

Creator and Sustainer,

we believe that you are love—
not merely loving, as if your love were
one attribute among many,
but love itself.

We believe that love defines the very essence of who you are,
that all your attributes are facets of this one thing:
others-oriented, self-giving, *kenotic* love.

And because you are love,
we know that we can trust you.

Because you are love,
we know that your heart is always for us,
and that your work in this world is always for our good.

We know that every good and perfect gift comes from you,
and that every evil is a deviation from your will.

But because you are love,
you do not force your will on anyone or anything.

Instead, you invite us to partner with you
so that your will may be done on earth as it is in heaven.

And when we partner with you,
you lead us into new and better ways of being.

This is what we desire, Lord.

We thank you for your invitation,
And we accept with gladness!

Help us to yield,
every day and every moment,
to your way of love.

PRAYER FOR THE BROKEN[7]
(BASED ON PSALM 34:18)

God, wherever we go, we walk among
those who hide unspeakable pain.
In our desire to give hope, help us to
create safe spaces for the hurting.
May this space also be a place where they
can seek help and share their pain.
Empower us to be Jesus to the broken.

**The Lord is close to the brokenhearted and
saves those who are crushed in spirit.**

We all have stories. Every story is important.
Our stories mold and form us.
Our stories break and transform us. God, help
us to value the stories each other holds.
Help us to create sacred spaces to hold those stories in safety.

**The Lord is close to the brokenhearted and
saves those who are crushed in spirit.**

Help us to be your tangible love through
the conscious choices we make.
Help us to courageously enter into the other's pain.
Help us wisely tell the victims that their
wounds were never part of your plan.
Allow us to share your love in creative ways.

**The Lord is close to the brokenhearted and
saves those who are crushed in spirit.**

Let us pray this prayer of dedication,
asking God's guidance for seeing others' brokenness
as our opportunity to show God's love.

(All)
**God, help me to see others for who they are
and not what has happened to them.
Help me to see their pain without judging their behavior.
Help me to act in ways that will be a bridge
of trust between you and the hurting.
Help me to hear your prompting,
demonstrate your active love,
and step into broken lives in ways that make a difference.
Help me to not control behavior in others
but instead love them to wholeness.
Allow me to speak hope into their lives.**

**We are the eyes that see the pain.
We are the feet who walk beside.
We are the ears that listen.
We are the arms that hold them as they heal.
The Lord is close to the brokenhearted and
saves those who are crushed in spirit.
Amen.**

PRAYER FOR SHALOM[8]

God of all people, places, and situations,
we come to you in prayer as forgiven people
seeking your strength and peace.
We have come to hear your wisdom as
we bring our petitions to you.
In this time of prayer, enlarge our capacity for love.
Sharpen our vision so that we may faithfully work
for the well-being of all your people
and your world.

We pray for shalom for all of those who dwell on the margins
of the economic systems in every country
and who suffer the pain and anxiety that comes
with a minimal income or financial insecurity.
We pray for the vulnerable, for the elderly and the children,
and especially for those who are hungry or sick.
Help us to partner with you so that our
world will more and more
reflect the values of your kingdom.
We pray for the time when we all acknowledge
that there is enough for everyone
and when everything is shared so that all
are able to enjoy your creation fully.

We pray for peace, healing, and justice for
those struggling in war-torn countries,
those trying to survive, who are mourning or in
need of food, water, shelter, and medical help.
We pray for those fleeing such regions, especially
in _____and _____.
We pray that borders may be opened and
creative short- and long-term solutions
to difficult problems may be found.

We pray for courageous peacemakers, and for those
people and agencies who dedicate their lives, work,
and energy to alleviating suffering of any kind,
especially those in dangerous situations.
Keep them safe and bring peace with justice swiftly.
May your kingdom come in all its fullness and come soon.

We pray for world leaders, that they will act with integrity,
wisdom, and compassion for the common good.
Our world needs good leaders.
Raise up new peacemakers with courage who will
partner with you against all forms of evil.
Continue to transform us to be effective partners too,
demonstrating your love, forgiveness,
and hope wherever we may go.
Amen.

PRAYER FOR A PERSON WITH LIFE-THREATENING ILLNESS[9]

Loving and Compassionate God,
we come seeking healing and wholeness for _____.
We know that you are with _____ in her/his pain.
We know that you seek healing even when a cure is unlikely.
May _____ experience your
companionship, grace, and healing touch.
May _____ know that her/his life is in your loving care
and that nothing can separate her/him from
your love in this life and the next.
Inspire us as friends and family to love deeply
and to share that love with _____.
Open our hearts and hands that we might bring,
by our presence, healing to her/his life.
Bless _____ and those who suffer,
and enable us to be instruments of peace
and healing to all we meet.
In Christ's name.
Amen.

PRAYER FOLLOWING A NATURAL DISASTER[10]

God of All Creation,
we see the devastation brought on by
_____, and our hearts are broken.
We feel powerless to help those who are homeless
and hopeless in _____'s wake.
We are tempted to stand on the sidelines
when your children need our help.
We can become overwhelmed by the immensity of need
and the realities of climate change that
have magnified the storm.
Wake us up, O Loving One, to the needs of others.
Inspire us to move from apathy to
empathy and passivity to agency.
Remind us that we are your companions,
that we are your heart and hands,
your wisdom and advocacy amidst the challenges of our world.
Awaken us to the power you have given us already,
and inspire us to claim greater powers of healing
and compassion in companionship with you
that we might truly be your partners in healing the Earth.
In Christ's name.
Amen.

PRAYER FOR A STRUGGLING FAMILY[11]

Lord God, you know every heart and are
intimate with all the challenges we face.
We lift up to you a family in our church who
is struggling and has requested prayer.
We know you have intimate knowledge
of all they are going through.
We thank you for working to bring good
out of every bad happening.
Thank you also for your constant presence with them,
strengthening, comforting, and upholding each one.
May they recognize you are suffering with
them until this situation is overcome.
In the name of Jesus,
Amen.

PRAYER OF THANKSGIVING[12]

We come humbly before you, the Uncontrolling God of Love.
We give you thanks.
Your grace is sufficient, even in our darkest hour.
Your hope is the candle within us that never fades.
We give you thanks.
When we see the chaos all around us, your
fierce love reminds us to carry on.
When we grow tired and weary, you
birth within us a new song.
You never allow death, oppression, and
hatred to be the last word.
Your love is endless, your justice relentless.
We give you thanks.
You asked us to join you on a sacred mission,
to spread love throughout the land.
We are your feet, we are your eyes, we
are your ears and your hands.
What an honor it is to represent your name.
To bring good news to the poor and witness
you deliver them from shame.
May you continue to teach us how to be
a community that is grateful.
**God, you are good. Your mercy and
compassion endure forever.
Your heart for justice is unwavering. We give you thanks.
Amen.**

PRAYER FOR REDEMPTIVE PARTNERSHIP[13]

Great God, amazing beyond comprehension
and yet willing to partner with humanity,
created in your image.

Continue to persuade us with your prevenient grace,
made new moment by moment,
as we learn more about who you are and how to be like you.

Provide for our needs in community
that we may be satisfied
but never grow too comfortable or
mistake frivolity for necessity.

Forgive us for failing to recognize privilege,
and show us how to be your redemptive agents in the world.

Give us courage to act as advocates
for those who have no voice—for the oppressed,
the marginalized, and the persecuted.

Help us to overcome our unbelief,
holding fast to a faith that recognizes
your work in all of creation
and your covenant with your people.

Make clear the most loving action in all things,
that we might join you in the labor of
bringing the kingdom earthside.

We praise you for who you are and thank you
for what you have done, are doing, and will continue to do
in and through us.
Amen.

INVOCATION FOR CHAOTIC TIMES[14]

Come, Great Spirit, come.
Keep our feet firmly on the ground as
our heads touch the skies.
Keep our sight clear and our ears tuned
to voices different from our own.
Keep our words true and our hearts and minds ajar.
Keep our hands empty to fill them with
the needs that arise before us.
Keep our arms spread wide to embrace possibilities.
(Silence)
May our gifts be revealed to us in this time,
that we might do the most excellent actions in your world:
to gladden the hearts of human beings,
and protect the earth we live in;
to fill the hungry, lift up the afflicted, lighten the
sorrowful, free the fearful, release the suffering.
(Silence)
Empower and encourage us, Gracious Spirit,
that we may liberate that which has been
given to us for the good of the whole
so that justice and joy might come to this great world,
so that we would complete the circle
that is your goodness in life.
(Silence)
Come, Generous Spirit, come shine on us and
through us on this day and all days,
that we might step out in courage and in love. May it be so.
Amen.

PRAYER FOR MERCY AND FORGIVENESS[15]

God, instead of becoming your agents of mercy and forgiveness,
we, like many of the Pharisees of Jesus's day, find it all too
easy to see the rest of the world as sinners who are under your
fierce judgment and ourselves as righteous and loved by you.
Grant us your divine ability to love
others in the midst of their sin.

Remind us in this very moment
that your relationship with others, and
our relationship with you
is forever based upon your love and acceptance.
Period.
(Silence)

Holy Spirit, remind us in this very moment
that it is not our right beliefs or behavior in
conformity with some moral code
or theological doctrine that causes you to love us.
You simply love us because you are Love.
(Silence)

Help us live in an almost constant state of repentance,
turning back to you and away from all of those
things that so easily capture our attention.
It is only as we repent and turn back to you, entering
a state of prayer and presence, that we experience the
great mystery of your mercy, forgiveness, and love.
Amen.

A PRAYER TO CO-GARDEN[16]

Cultivating God,
you are the ultimate source of growth and
transformation in the world.
Thank you for giving clothing to the flowers of
the fields and breathing life into the soil.
We ask that you be the light that warms
our relationship with the ground.
Help us to be gardeners and caregivers of the earth,
that all earth's seeds might be fruitful and feed a hungry world.
May we tread tenderly on the face of the earth with love,
compassion, and mindfulness of each
other and the rest of creation.
In all your infinite names we pray,
Amen.

PRAYER FOR PEACE: A LITANY[17]

Gracious God, Creator of all truth and beauty,
all peace and justice,
you have created all humanity in your image—
all of us bear your fingerprints on our lives,
and you have declared all creation to be good.

But this world has become something other
than what you created it to be.
Instead of love and peace, compassion and grace,
our hearts and hands have contributed to
hatred and conflict,
apathy and judgment.
We have substituted arrogance for humility,
vengeance for forgiveness,
selfishness for service.

Yet, for some reason beyond our ability to comprehend,
you are here, now, in the midst of it all—
in the midst of all our self-made chaos.

How can that be?
How is it that you, the One who is *above*
all, freely chooses to be *in* all—
in all the muck and mire of your creation that has gone astray?

God, we long for peace.

Help us to understand that
although you do not cause everything,
you desire good to come from all that happens.

When we are tempted to contribute to discord,
give us steady feet and calm minds.
When we marginalize, abuse, or steal hope,
turn our hearts and minds toward shalom—
that which is not simply the absence of conflict and injustice
but is also the presence of wholeness,
well-being, and goodness—
to thereby become vehicles of your transforming grace.

God, may we be your hands that work for peace.

Even in the midst of darkness and chaos where we do not see it,
you are at work.
You have the power to create beauty through us—
out of the mess we have created.

Give us patience as we work with you.
Gently but firmly restrain us from rushing ahead of you.
As we partner with you, let us see the ugliness in ourselves
and in our world
so that we can transform it
rather than draw a veil over it.

God, help us be your agents of peace.

Keep us from all apathy and hubris.
Let our hearts love so strongly
that they break time and time again
at the sight of unrest.

Let us never be content simply to be peacekeepers,
but let us always work toward being peacemakers
so that our zeal for peace grows brighter and stronger
with each passing day.

Let our hearts be seedbeds,
our minds be drawing boards,
and our hands be instruments
of your peace in the world.

God, sustain us in the work of peacemaking.

Finally, Lord God, we offer this prayer
not for peace "one day"
but for peace now and every day.

Beginning with me.

O God, we will be your partners in peace.
Amen.

PRAYER OF CON-SPIRING[18]

O God who is above us and below us, around us
and inside us with each breath we take,
we thank you for the Breath of Life.
From the very beginning we are told,
your Breath, your *ruah*, your presence enlivens the world and
brings all of creation to life.

All creatures exchange your Breath with the trees and plants,
thousands of times each day,
con-spiring together, breathing together,
participating in an interspecies ritual of communion with you,
reminding us of the sacred gift of life.

We have been taught to recognize the body and blood of Christ
in the everyday world of grains and grapes.
May we now learn to sense your presence
in every breath we take
so that we understand that
when we dirty the air,
when our actions make it so others cannot easily breathe,
when we make the creation warm too much,
we stifle your presence, we defile the Breath.

Let us vow that in our life's limit of breaths
we make it so no one has to say, "I can't breathe."
Let us vow that in our life's limit of breaths
our breathmates, the trees, can live and thrive.

O God of Breath,
may each breath we take together—
our con-spiring with each other and the forest—
may it clear our minds and hearts.
May it enliven our vision with justice and compassion.
May it reconnect us with the creation
so that we strive to truly live in communion
with all living beings on this one earth.

And so, with each breath—
(breathing prayer)
YAHHH WEHHH
YAHHH WEHHH
—we remember that life is sacred.

PRAYER TO THE PILGRIM GOD[19]

Pilgrim God, you journey with us,
coming alongside,
walking our path.

**Thank you for loving us
and not leaving us alone.
Thank you for caring about our paths
and not leaving us helpless.**

We confess
sometimes we wish you would just get us to the destination.
Sometimes we wish you would at least fix the path.
Sometimes we yearn to not see through a glass darkly.

**This journey is hard.
So much is broken.
We're not sure of how our story unfolds into Yours.**

Sometimes we wish you would do the walking for us.
Sometimes we wish you were not a Pilgrim God.
Sometimes we're not sure we want to be a pilgrim people.

**Yet you faithfully journey with us,
coming alongside, walking our path**

You invite us to faithfully journey with others when it is hard.
You show us how to come alongside
those who suffer brokenness,
walking with those who feel sidelined.

Pilgrim God,
we welcome you and join you as pilgrim people.
We commit to being like you,
walking the path of love and justice for all.
Amen.

INDIVIDUAL PRAYERS

The following individual prayers by various authors, scholars, and laypersons are examples of "conspiring prayer" and are grounded in God's uncontrolling love, issues of social justice, and human partnership.

PRAYER OF COMMITMENT[1]

God of the entire universe and friend to me,
I look to you again today to be my guide.
I will listen for your still, small voice.
I will heed the gentle nudges, the intuitions,
and the positive insights that arise.
I commit myself, once again, to live a life of love.
Help me discern how I might love well today.
Give me wisdom and sensitivity.
I commit myself to respond creatively to your calls.
I commit myself to pursue justice, right living, and generosity.
In light of the needs I see next to me and
those I know of in the wider world,
I commit to responding to your leading.
I will love you, love others, and love myself.
I commit myself, once again, to live a life of love.
Amen.

COME LORD JESUS[2]

Friend of Sinners, friend of mine, thank you.
Thank you for so much—for you, for me, for my life,
for my family, and for my friends.
Thank you for your provision, for your
guidance, for your wisdom.
Thank you for making me—for dreaming me into
existence and inviting me into your great rescue
mission to redeem the world back to yourself.
For so long I have lived for myself—for my
dreams and my desires and my well-being—
but today I commit myself to living for you—for your dreams,
for your desires, and for the well-being of all of humanity.
Help me today to be you to those who cross my path.
When people look into my eyes, may they see you.
When they hear my words, may they hear you.
When they feel my touch or my embrace, may they feel you.
May my words today inspire and challenge
and build up and push forward.
May they give hope, show grace, and exhibit mercy.
May they bring heaven ever closer to earth.
Come, Lord Jesus.
Come into my life afresh today
so that I might carry you into the lives of others.
Amen.

DEAR SOUL FRIEND[3]

So often, I wish I were a better friend to you.
I get so distracted, so preoccupied with my concerns.
I'm so busy inwardly and outwardly.
I can't stay still long enough just to reach out and
touch you and let you touch me, too—
almost like we were at a coffee shop together.
I am not afraid of you. I love you and long to be closer to you.
Perhaps sometimes you long to be closer to me, too?
Do you ever get lonely?
Do you ever wish you could just relax a
little, like on the seventh day?

I fear that "church" may be part of the problem.
Sometimes when I am in church listening
to music that praises you,
I feel like I am at a pep rally and that we are
cheering for you so that you might love us.
I don't think you want or need our cheering.
It may even embarrass you a little.
There's a humility in your style; you don't
mind living in the shadows a bit.
But I think you want our friendship—not for
our sake alone but for your sake, too.

I am told by open and relational theologians
that you can't and won't control us.
They say that your power is of a different
sort: luring, empowering, guiding.
I'm glad about that. But I'm guessing you grow a
little weary of exercising all of the uncontrolling
power on your own, without our help.

You must be so busy. I want to help you rest.
I know a little place on Third and Main;
it's called Seventh Day Coffee Shop.
I'll meet you there.

You've given me so much over these years:
your love, your forgiveness, your humor,
your power, your playfulness, your guidance, your hope.
You are so strong, but maybe a little lonesome.
How about this time I give something back?
10 a.m. sound good?
It's my treat.

EVENING PRAYER FOR THOSE IMPRISONED[4]

Jesus.
Savior. Brother. Friend.
Guard my soul in this cell of night.
Defend me from self-injuring doubt and debilitating fear.
Gift me with the sleep that heals.

May those I have harmed forgive me.
May those who've injured me be forgiven.
I ask this in your name—you who knew no sin.

Jesus, be Savior, Brother, and Friend
to those who are lost
or locked away from your love.
Soften the hearts of those who condemn.
Strengthen the lives of all who long for freedom.

When morning comes, may mourning end.
Bend the bars of death.
Help me rise and praise you.
Let me see the sun,
my Savior, Brother, and Friend.
Amen.

PERSONAL PRAYER FOR
THE DAY AHEAD[5]

You have invited Christ-followers to actively partner with you
and with others who share your values. I accept that invitation.
I pray that as I journey with you throughout this day,
your Spirit will enable me to be more like you.
I pray that I will be gracious as you are gracious,
forgiving as you are forgiving, and
generous as you are generous.
Help me be continually aware of your
presence and activity in the world,
and embolden me to witness to your faithfulness and love.
May I be an authentic ambassador of you and your kingdom.
May all that I say and do reflect your character and
be appropriate activities of your kingdom.
I ask all this in the authority of Jesus, the Christ.
Amen.

MEDITATIVE PRAYERS AND REFLECTIONS

The following meditative prayers and reflections by various authors, scholars, and laypersons are examples of "conspiring prayer" and are grounded in God's uncontrolling love, issues of social justice, and human partnership.

MEDITATIVE REFLECTION FOR AN INVITATION TO PRAYER[1]

(One can use jazz underneath—sax and drums)

Silence, nothingness, in the darkness.
Silence, waiting to be broken.
Yearning, reaching out, touching.
A note, a beat, a sound.
And the vast heavenly host stands still
as the rising comes, not yet spoken,
breaking, calling, luring,
a sense of wonder rising,
rising out of the earth.

In the garden of the rising sky,
can you see, coming through the fission of
the earth, along the water ways,
the movement of rising, the sky of peace,
the sky of mercy, the sky of love,
the sky of memory and sharing,
the sky of blessed life, seeking completion?
Wholeness, healing, sky full of light.

God's dreaming,
calling over the chaos, the beginnings of life rising.
Listen to the intensity, listen to the harmony.
The cry of love.
From the inner imagination, from the edge of experience,
love comes tumbling down.
Like a watcher at the moment of dawn,
love comes to us
uninvited, without our calling, overtaking us.
This grand creation,
this global, circling transformation,
this heart-stopping beauty,
bringing together all that is and will be.
We are there, in that moment, standing
at the tomb on tiptoes, looking
through the veil to the rising,
feeling the touch of love,
feeling the love in our souls.
No longer distracted,
our pores are open.
Our heart is open.

Silence.

ART AND RELIGION: A PRAYER OF ALTERNATE DEFINITIONS[2]

(Slowly read and internalize each definition.
This in itself can become a meditation.)

art: complexity held in delicate tension; exploration of matters of ultimate concern

artwork: a worldview made manifest

beauty: a harkening to the wholeness of Eden; the bringing about of shalom

creation: collaboration, relational emergence; productive interdependence

knowing: acquaintance with the unknowable

meaning: elucidation of relations, interconnections, implications, contingencies

observation: imagining from within another's worldview; empathy training

openness: finding self in the other; receiving the other as self; active passivity toward the Divine Other.

truth: the intersection of worldviews

religion: complexity held in delicate tension; exploration of matters of ultimate concern

(Pray the prayer below in its entirety or focus on any one stanza, line, or word:
  1. Read as written.
  2. Substitute words for their above definitions.)

3. *Read again using new definitions. Spend time with each combination.*
4. *Meditate on new meanings, new outcomes, new implications, new consequences, new actions.*
5. *Pray for the Spirit's prodding.*
6. *Return to prayer over time as desired until you feel all meditations are exhausted.)*

Relational God,

may our religion birth our artwork,
may our artwork encourage observation,
may our observation motivate creation.

May our creation generate meaning,
may our meaning foster openness,
may our openness enact truth.

May our truth produce knowing,
may our knowing beget beauty,
may our beauty be our art, our religion.

May it be so. Amen.

(If / when all meditations are exhausted, consider the given combinations above. Reconsider, recombine, rewrite, redefine; discover new relations. Pray for the Spirit's prodding. Test each new combination against the Spirit's prodding. Meditate on new meanings, new outcomes, new implications, new consequences, new actions.)

A Prayer[3]

O God, I am counted among those who dwell in hell, for I have forsaken the inexhaustible fountain of Your Word. Guide us now to be strong, to have understanding, that wherever there is a length to the days, or wherever there is life, we might find Holy Wisdom with Your Light and Your Peace.

May we be turned toward Her, for She has lived among us and has commanded the leopards of the mountains; She is the Law and Commandments of the people of old. May we be drawn to Her Light, and may that Light live in our hearts and be spoken on our lips.

Living within us, we have intermixed the bread and wine, which She has offered to us, so our footsteps may be guided by Her Light, our tongues be the language of justice and righteousness, and Her Wisdom perfume every tomb and ambry we liberate, and bestow upon the humble the fullness of Her treasures of Love.

Amen.

Proverbs 8, Song of Songs 4, Baruch 3

ENDNOTES

INTRODUCTION

1. Dallas Willard, *The Divine Conspiracy* (London: William Collins, 1998), 268–69.

2. Thomas Jay Oord, *The Uncontrolling Love of God: An Open and Relational Account of Providence* (Downers Grove, IL: InterVarsity Press, 2016).

3. Oord, *Uncontrolling*, 183.

4. Another term for *unilateral* is *single-handedly*. I will use both interchangeably throughout the book.

5. Oord, *Uncontrolling*, 200.

CHAPTER 1

1. Lee Strobel, *The Case for Christ: A Journalist's Personal Investigation of the Evidence for Jesus* (Grand Rapids: Zondervan, 1998), under heading *Judging for Yourself*, paragraph 6.

2. Louis J. Cozolino, *The Neuroscience of Human Relationships: Attachment and the Developing Social Brain* (New York: Norton, 2006), 410–11.

3. John T. Cacioppo and William Patrick, *Loneliness: Human Nature and the Need for Social Connection* (New York: Norton, 2008), 92.

4. Naomi I. Eisenberger, Matthew D. Lieberman, and Kipling D. Williams, "Does Rejection Hurt?: An fMRI Study of Social Exclusion," *Science* 302 (2003): 290–92.

5. Charles Foster, *The Sacred Journey* (Nashville, TN: Nelson, 2010), 163.

6. Martin E. Marty, *Martin Luther: A Life* (New York: Viking, 2004), 16.

7. Evans, Rachel Held. Searching for Sunday: loving, leaving, and finding the Church. (Nashville: Thomas Nelson Inc, 2015), 51-52.

8. Dr. Chris Boesel, Systematic Theology Class, Drew University, 2010.

9. Philip Zaleski and Carol Zaleski, *Prayer: A History* (Boston: Houghton Mifflin, 2005), 4.

10. Herbert Benson and Marg Stark, *Timeless Healing: The Power and Biology of Belief* (New York: Simon & Schuster, 1997), 196.

11. Walter Brueggemann, *Great Prayers of the Old Testament* (Louisville: Westminster John Knox, 2008), xi.

12. Glynn Cardy, "A Progressive Christian Understanding of Prayer," in *Wisdom and Imagination: Religious Progressives and the Search for Meaning*, eds. Rex A. E. Hunt and Gregory C. Jenks (Northcote, VIC: Morning Star, 2014), 133.

13. Bruce Ellis Benson and Norman Wirzba, *The Phenomenology of Prayer* (New York: Fordham University Press, 2005), 218.

14. Origen, *Origen: An Exhortation to Martyrdom, Prayer, and Selected Works*, trans. Rowan A. Greer (New York: Paulist, 1979), 92.

15. C. S. Lewis and Walter Hooper, *Christian Reflections* (Grand Rapids: Eerdmans, 1967), 142–51.

16. Sybil MacBeth, *Praying in Color: Drawing a New Path to God* (Brewster, MA: Paraclete Press, 2007) 48.

17. John Ortberg, *Faith & Doubt* (Grand Rapids: Zondervan, 2008), 31.

CHAPTER 2

1. Edward M. Bounds, *Power Through Prayer* (Chicago: Moody, 2009), 102–103.

2. Oord, *Uncontrolling*.

CHAPTER 3

1. See Lauren Haas, *A Philosophical Analysis of Petitionary Prayer* (PhD diss., Baylor University, 2012). You can access it at: https://baylor-ir.tdl. org/baylor-ir/bitstream/handle/2104/8713/Paige_Haas_HonorsThesis. pdf?sequence=1.

2. Scott A. Davison, *Petitionary Prayer: A Philosophical Investigation* (Oxford: Oxford University Press, 2017), 157.

3. Oord, *Uncontrolling*.

4. Gregory A. Boyd, *Crucifixion of the Warrior God: Volumes 1 & 2* (Minneapolis: Augsburg Fortress, 2017), 491–92.

5. Paul Fiddes, *Participating in God: A Pastoral Doctrine of the Trinity* (London: Darton, Longman & Todd, 2000), 139.

6. C. Robert Mesle, *Process Theology: A Basic Introduction* (Atlanta: Chalice, 1993), 39.

7. Bruce R. Reichenbach, *Divine Providence: God's Love and Human Freedom* (Eugene, OR: Cascade, 2016), 249.

8. Isaac Choi, "Is Petitionary Prayer Superfluous?" in *Oxford Studies in Philosophy of Religion*, vol. 7, ed. Jonathan Kvanvig (Oxford: Oxford University Press, 2016), 41.

9. Paul Copan, *Loving Wisdom: Christian Philosophy of Religion* (Atlanta: Chalice, 2007), 42.

10. Peter Vardy and Charlotte Vardy, *God Matters* (London: SCM, 2013), 200.

11. Georges Rey, "Meta-atheism: Religious Avowal as Self-Deception," in *Philosophers without Gods: Meditations on Atheism and the Secular Life*, ed. Louise M. Anthony (Oxford: Oxford University Press, 2007), 261.

12. Jerome Gellman, "Judaic Perspectives on Petitionary Prayer," in *Referring to God: Jewish and Christian Philosophical and Theological Perspectives*, ed. Paul Helm (New York: Routledge, 2011), 129–48.

13. Oord, *Uncontrolling*, 89.

14. Bruce Epperly, *Praying with Process Theology: Spiritual Practices for Personal and Planetary Healing* (Anoka, MN: River Lane Press, 2017), 17.

15. Vincent Brümmer, *What Are We Doing When We Pray? On Prayer and the Nature of Faith* (Farnham, Surrey, UK: Ashgate, 2008), 64.

16. Brümmer, *What Are We Doing When We Pray?*, 64.

17. Michael J. Murray, "Does God Respond to Prayer?" in *Contemporary Debates in Philosophy of Religion*, eds. Michael L. Peterson and Raymond J. VanArragon (Malden, MA: Blackwell, 2004), 242–55, here 251.

18. David Basinger, "God Does Not Necessarily Respond to Prayer," in *Contemporary Debates in Philosophy of Religion*, ed. Michael L. Peterson and Raymond J. VanArragon (Malden, MA: Blackwell Publishers, 2004), 255-263, here 255.

19. Edward M. Bounds, *The Possibilities of Prayer* (New York: Fleming H. Revell, 1923).

20. Josian Frampton, *Pray and Watch the Impossible Happen* (Sarasota, FL: First Edition Design, 2014), 8.

21. Gregory A. Boyd, *God at War: The Bible & Spiritual Conflict* (Downers Grove, IL: InterVarsity Press, 1997), 205.

CHAPTER 4

1. "God Isn't Fixing This," *The New York Daily News*, December 3, 2015.

2. James W. Basinger and Paige A. Nunnelley, "Private Prayer Associations with Depression, Anxiety and Other Health Conditions: An Analytical Review of Clinical Studies," *Postgraduate Medicine* 128 (2016): 635–41.

3. Stephanie Winkel, John Black, Patrick Pössel, Benjamin D. Jeppsen, Annie C. Bjerg, and Don T. Wooldridge, "Disclosure During Private Prayer as a Mediator Between Prayer Type and Mental Health in an Adult Christian Sample," *Journal of Religion and Health* 54 (2015): 540–53.

4. Winkel et al., "Disclosure During Private Prayer," 549.

5. Winkel et al., "Disclosure During Private Prayer," 549.

6. Ann Riesselman Struve, Der-Fa Lu, Laura Hart, and Theresa Keller, "The Use of Intercessory Prayer to Reduce Disruptive Behaviors of Patients with Dementia: A Pilot Feasibility Study," *Journal of Holistic Nursing: Official Journal of the American Holistic Nurses' Association* 34 (2016):135–45, doi: 10.1177/0898010115587400.

7. David R. Hodge, "A Systematic Review of the Empirical Literature on Intercessory Prayer," *Research on Social Work Practice* 17 (2007): 181.

8. David R. Hodge, "A Systematic Review of the Empirical Literature on Intercessory Prayer," *Research on Social Work Practice* 17 (2007): 183.

9. Ian Olver and Andrew Dutney, "A randomized, blinded study of the impact of intercessory prayer on spiritual well-being in patients with cancer," *Alternative Therapies in Health and Medicine*, 18 (2012): 18–27, doi: 10.1007/978-1-4614-4571-5_5.

10. Hodge, "A Systematic Review of the Empirical Literature on Intercessory Prayer," 185.

11. Kevin S. Masters, Glen I. Spielmans, and Jason T. Goodson, "Are There Demonstrable Effects of Distant Intercessory Prayer? A Meta-Analytic Review," *Annals of Behavioral Medicine* 32 (2006): 25.

12. Richard P. Sloan, *Blind Faith: The Unholy Alliance of Religion and Medicine* (New York: St. Martin's Press, 2006), 176.

13. Herbert Benson, Jeffery A. Dusek, Jane B. Sherwood, Peter Lam, Charles F. Bethea, William Carpenter, Patricia L Hibberd, et al., "Study of the Therapeutic Effects of Intercessory Prayer (STEP) in Cardiac Bypass Patients: A Multicenter Randomized Trial of Uncertainty and Certainty of Receiving Intercessory Prayer," *American Heart Journal* 151 (2006): 934–42.

14. Claudia Kalb, "Don't Pray for Me! Please!" *Newsweek* 147 (April 10, 2006).

15. Tomas James Rees, "Is Personal Insecurity a Cause of Cross-National Differences in the Intensity of Religious Belief?" *Journal of Religion and Society* 11 (2009): 12.

16. Sloan, *Blind Faith*, 171.

17. Harold G. Koenig, *Spirituality and Health Research: Methods, Measurements, Statistics, and Resources* (West Conshohocken, PA: Templeton Press, 2011), 183.

18. "About Sexual Assault," RAINN, accessed January 6, 2017, https://www.rainn.org/about-sexual-assault.

19. "Assault or Homicide" CDC, accessed July 6, 2017, https://www.cdc.gov/nchs/fastats/homicide.htm.

20. "Latest Hate Crime Statistics Released," FBI, November 14, 2016, https://www.fbi.gov/news/stories/2015-hate-crime-statistics-released.

21. "Intentional Fires," NFPA, accessed January 6, 2017, http://www.nfpa.org/news-and-research/fire-statistics-and-reports/fire-statistics/fire-causes/arson-and-juvenile-firesetting/intentional-fires.

22. "Larceny-theft," FBI, accessed January 6, 2017, https://ucr.fbi.gov/crime-in-the-u.s/2010/crime-in-the-u.s.-2010/property-crime/larcenytheftmain.

23. "The State of Homelessness in America," National Alliance to End Homelessness, accessed January 6, 2017, http://www.endhomelessness.org/library/entry/SOH2016.

24. "Annual Causes of Death in the United States," Drug War Facts, accessed January 6, 2017, http://www.drugwarfacts.org/cms/Causes_of_Death#sthash.ltJpIYWt.dpbs.

25. "Trends & Statistics," National Institute on Drug Abuse, accessed January 6, 2017, https://www.drugabuse.gov/related-topics/trends-statistics.

26. Helen L. Parish and William G. Naphy, *Religion and Superstition in Reformation Europe* (Manchester: Manchester University Press, 2002), 3.

27. Sybel MacBeth, *Praying in Color: Drawing a New Path to God* (Brewster, MA: Paraclete Press, 2013), 48.

28. Jack Corbin Getz, *Praying When Prayer Doesn't Work: Finding A Way Back to the Heart of God*, (Bloomington, IN: iUniverse, 2010), 53.

29. Getz, *Praying When Prayer Doesn't Work*, 53.

30. Cornelius Plantinga Jr., *Not the Way It's Supposed to Be: A Breviary of Sin* (Grand Rapids: Eerdmans, 1995), 10.

31. Karl Barth, *Church Dogmatics III. 3: The Doctrine of Creation* (London: T&T Clark, 2004), 264.

32. Amanda Murphey, "Catherine And Herbert Schaible, Pennsylvania Pentecostal Couple, Sentenced for Neglecting to Take Sick Son to Doctor," *The Huffington Post*, February 19, 2014, http://www.huffingtonpost.com/2014/02/19/catherine-herbert-schaible-sentence_n_4818659.html.

CHAPTER 5

1. Thomas L. Constable, *Talking to God: What the Bible Teaches about Prayer* (Grand Rapids: Baker Books, 1995), 51.

2. Robert W. Yarbrough, *1–3 John* (Grand Rapids: Baker Academic, 2008), 366.

3. Yarbrough, *1–3 John*, 366.

4. Wesley L. Duewel, *Mighty Prevailing Prayer: Experiencing the Power of Answered Prayer* (Grand Rapids: Zondervan, 1990), 233.

5. David Crump, *Knocking on Heaven's Door: A New Testament Theology of Petitionary Prayer* (Grand Rapids: Baker Academic, 2006), 62.

6. James Strong, *Strong's Exhaustive Concordance of the Bible*, updated and expanded ed. (Peabody, MA: Hendrickson, 2007), 1600.

7. Derek Prince, *The Holy Spirit in You* (New Kensington, PA: Whitaker House, 1987), 68.

8. Raymond F. Collins, *The Power of Images in Paul* (Collegeville, MN: Liturgical Press, 2008), 85.

9. Tony Evans, *Victory in Spiritual Warfare* (Eugene, OR: Harvest House, 2011), 140.

10. Boyd, *Crucifixion of the Warrior God*, 652.

11. Thomas J. Oord, *The Nature of Love: A Theology* (Atlanta: Chalice, 2010), 2.

12. Boyd, *Crucifixion of the Warrior God*, 652.

13. While I agree with some of Boyd's proposal, I do take issue with the phrase "God allowed." See Mark Karris, "Rethinking the Phrase 'God Allowed'," in *Uncontrolling Love: Essays Exploring the Love of God with Introductions by Thomas Jay Oord*, eds. Chris Baker, Gloria Coffin, Craig Drurey, Graden Kirksey, Lisa Michaels, Donna Fiser Ward (San Diego: SacraSage Press, 2017), 199–203.

14. Boyd, *Crucifixion of the Warrior God*, 511.

15. Boyd, *Crucifixion of the Warrior God*, xxxiv.

16. Lawrence O. Richards, *The Bible Reader's Companion: Your Guide to Every Chapter of the Bible* (Colorado Springs: David C. Cook, 1991), 235.

17. Robert L. Plummer, *40 Questions About Interpreting the Bible* (Grand Rapids: Kregel, 2010), 38.

18. "Infallible," *Dictionary.com Unabridged* (Random House), accessed December 30, 2017, http://www.dictionary.com/browse/infallible.

19. Ian Howard Marshall, *The Acts of the Apostles: An Introduction and Commentary* (Grand Rapids: Eerdmans, 1980), 209.

20. Richard Longenecker, quoted in Robert L. Gallagher and Paul Hertig, eds. *Mission in Acts: Ancient Narratives in Contemporary Context* (Maryknoll, NY: Orbis Books, 2004), 162–63.

21. F. F. Bruce, *The Book of the Acts* (Grand Rapids: Eerdmans, 1988), 236.

22. John R. W. Stott, *The Message of Acts: To the Ends of the Earth* (Leicester: Inter-Varsity Press, 1994), 103.

23. John B. Weaver, *Plots of Epiphany: Prison-escape in Acts of the Apostles* (Berlin: de Gruyter, 2004), 286.

24. Josep Rius-Camps and Jenny Read-Heimerdinger, *The Message of Acts in Codex Bezae: A Comparison with the Alexandrian Tradition*, vol. 2 (London: T&T Clark, 2004), 340.

25. See Carol A. Newsom and Brennan W. Breed, *Daniel: A Commentary* (Louisville: Westminster John Knox, 2014), 2.

26. John J. Collins, *The Apocalyptic Imagination: An Introduction to Jewish Apocalyptic Literature* (Grand Rapids: Eerdmans, 1998), 21.

27. Stephen L. Cook, *The Apocalyptic Literature* (Nashville: Abingdon, 2003), 67.

28. I am trying to resist a complete spiritual/earth dichotomy.

29. Craig A. Evans, *The Bible Knowledge Background Commentary: Matthew–Luke, Volume 1* (Colorado Springs: Victor Books, 2003), 169.

30. See Robert H. Gundry, *A Survey of the New Testament*, 5th ed. (Grand Rapids: Zondervan, 2012), 204–205.

CHAPTER 6

1. As quoted in Mark Casto, *When Misfits Become Kings: Unlock Your Future through Intimacy with God* (Lake Mary, FL: Charisma House, 2015), 83.

2. Norman Pittenger, *The Holy Spirit* (Philadelphia, PA: Pilgrim Press, 1974), 17.

3. Peter Rollins, *How (Not) to Speak of God* (Brewster, MA: Paraclete Press, 2006), 49.

4. Rollins, *How (Not) to Speak of God*, 49.

5. Leonard I. Sweet, *Nudge: Awakening Each Other to the God Who's Already There* (Colorado Springs: David C. Cook, 2010), 50.

6. Sweet, *Nudge*, 50.

7. Oord, *Uncontrolling*, 202.

8. Oord, *Uncontrolling*, 190.

9. Oord, *Uncontrolling*, 94.

10. Philip Yancey, *Prayer: Does it Make any Difference?* (London: Hodder & Stoughton, 2006), 208.

11. Oord, *Uncontrolling*, 181.

12. Oord, *Uncontrolling*, 170.

13. Thomas G. Belt, *A Critical Evaluation of the Religious Adequacy of Open Theism: Toward an Open Theistic Theology of Petitionary Prayer* (MA diss., University of Wales, 2007).

14. Oord, *Uncontrolling*, 148.

15. Oord, *Uncontrolling*, 148.

16. William Hasker, *God, Time, and Knowledge* (Ithaca, NY: Cornell University Press, 1989), 196, author's italics removed.

17. William Paul Young, *The Shack: Where Tragedy Confronts Eternity* (Newbury Park, CA: Windblown Media, 2007), 165.

18. William Hasker, *The Triumph of God Over Evil: Theodicy for a World of Suffering* (Downers Grove, IL: InterVarsity Press, 2008), 125.

19. Kenneth K. Pak, *Divine Power and Evil: A Reply to Process Theodicy* (London: Routledge, 2016), 171.

20. Jean-Paul Sartre, *Being and Nothingness* (New York: Pocket Books, 1984), 278.

21. Kevin Moore, *God, Conceivability, and Evil: The Logical Problem of Evil Revisited* (Crestwood, KY: Meta House, 2017), 43.

22. Moore, *God, Conceivability, and Evil*, 43.

CHAPTER 7

1. Mark Karris, *Season of Heartbreak: Healing for the Heart, Brain, and Soul* (Grand Rapids: Kregel, 2017), 147.

2. "Control," *Oxford Dictionary of English*, 3rd ed. (Oxford: Oxford University Press, 2010).

3. Oord, *Uncontrolling*, 213.

4. David Basinger, "God Does Not Necessarily Respond to Prayer," in *Contemporary Debates in Philosophy of Religion*, ed. Michael L. Peterson and Raymond J. VanArragon (Malden, MA: Blackwell Publishers, 2004), 255–64.

5. Basinger, "God Does Not Necessarily Respond to Prayer," 261.

6. Chris Band, *On My Knees: Rebuilding Our Confidence in Prayer* (Oxford: Monarch Books, 2016), 85.

7. Although the translators of the NIV (along with some other translations) used the English verb "relent" in this verse (as well as Exodus 32:14 and Jonah 3:10), they used "change his mind" in Numbers 23:19, which uses the same Hebrew verb. Note that the KJV consistently uses "repent" in all these cases. The translators' goal in using different English verbs in this case was to avoid any sense that the Bible was contradicting itself. But, it is proper contextualized interpretation that prevents such a contradiction, not sleight of hand by a translator. Regardless of whether the violent portrayals of God in the Hebrew Bible are accurate, one thing is clear: the biblical writers depicted God as one who could change his mind.

8. Bruce Epperly, *Process Theology: A Guide for the Perplexed* (London: T&T Clark, 2011), 58.

9. Marjorie Suchocki, *In God's Presence: Theological Reflections on Prayer* (Atlanta: Chalice, 1996), 46-48.

10. Kathleen Fischer, *Reclaiming the Connections: A Contemporary Spirituality* (Kansas City: Sheed & Ward, 1990), 23.

11. Philip Clements-Jewery, *Intercessory Prayer: Modern Theology, Biblical Teaching and Philosophical Thought* (Farnham, Surrey, UK: Ashgate, 2016), 134.

12. Clements-Jewery, *Intercessory Prayer*, 143.

13. Oord, *Uncontrolling*, 42.

CHAPTER 8

1. "Conspire," *Merriam-Webster's Collegiate Dictionary*, 11th ed. (Springfield, MA: Merriam-Webster, 2004), 267.

2. Martin Buber, *I and Thou*, trans. Walter Kaufmann (New York: Scribner's Sons, 1970), 131.

3. John Stott, *The Message of Romans: God's Good News for the World* (Downers Grove, IL: InterVarsity Press, 1994), 245.

4. Samuel C. Williamson, *Hearing God in Conversation: How to Recognize His Voice Everywhere* (Grand Rapids: Kregel, 2016), 18.

5. Leonard I. Sweet and Frank Viola, *Jesus Speaks: Learning to Recognize and Respond to the Lord's Voice* (Nashville: W Publishing Group, 2016), 152.

6. N. T. Wright, *The Day the Revolution Began: Reconsidering the Meaning of Jesus's Crucifixion* (San Francisco: HarperOne, 2016), Kindle edition, ch. 14, "Rethinking Mission," paragraph 4.

7. Leonard Sweet, *So Beautiful: Divine Design for Life and the Church* (Colorado Springs: David C. Cook, 2009), 55.

8. Henri J. M. Nouwen, *With Open Hands* (Notre Dame, IN: Ave Maria Press, 1972), 44.

9. Barbie Latza Nadeau, Milena Veselinovic, Madison Park, and Laura Smith-Spark, "Italy avalanche: 7 survivors rescued from buried hotel," *CNN*, January 20, 2017, http://www.cnn.com/2017/01/20/europe/italy-avalanche-earthquake/index.html.

10. David G. Benner, "Why Pray?" September 17, 2017, http://www.drdavidgbenner.ca/why-pray/.

11. Benner, "Why Pray?"

12. Benner, "Why Pray?"

13. Quoted by Diane Bishop, "'Prayer changes us and we change things,'" October 13, 2015, http://www.harvbishop.com/?p=251.

14. As quoted in Michael Frost and Christiana Rice, *To Alter Your World: Partnering with God to Rebirth Our Communities.* (Downers Grove: InterVarsity Press, 2017), 114.

15. Shane Claiborne and Jonathan Wilson-Hartgrove, *Becoming the Answer to Our Prayers: Prayer for Ordinary Radicals* (Downers Grove, IL: InterVarsity Press, 2008), 117.

CHAPTER 9

1. Hasker, *The Triumph of God Over Evil*, 163.

2. Howard Thurman, *Essential Writings*, ed. Luther E. Smith, Jr. (Maryknoll, NY: Orbis Books, 2006), 58.

3. The Leapfrog Group, "Five Years After the Launch of the Leapfrog Hospital Safety Grade, Patient Safety Improves, But Crucial Work Remains," April 12, 2017, http://www.leapfroggroup.org/news-events/five-years-after-launch-leapfrog-hospital-safety-grade-patient-safety-improves-crucial.

4. Katie Rogers, "At Least 27 Shot, 7 Fatally, in Chicago Over Christmas Weekend," *The New York Times*, December 25, 2016, http://www.nytimes.com/2016/12/25/us/chicago-shootings-gun-violence.html?_r=0.

5. Luther E. Smith Jr's introduction to *Howard Thurman: Essential Writings*, by Howard Thurman (Maryknoll, NY: Orbis Books, 2006), 59.

6. Tamar Manasseh, private Facebook message to author, December 26, 2016.

7. Aimee Levitt, "The Rabbinic Student with a Plan to Solve Chicago's Gun Violence Problem," *The Forward*, December 5, 2016, http://forward.com/news/national/356057/the-rabbinic-student-with-a-plan-to-solve-chicagos-gun-violence-problem/. Courtesy of Tamar Manasseh.

8. "Why Chicago hasn't yet escaped an epidemic of gun violence," *PBS NewsHour*, September 7, 2016, http://www.pbs.org/newshour/bb/chicago-hasnt-yet-escaped-epidemic-gun-violence/.

9. Quoted in Chris Band, *On My Knees: Rebuilding Our Confidence in Prayer* (Oxford: Monarch Books, 2016), 22.

10. Marjorie Suchocki, *God Christ Church: A Practical Guide to Process Theology* (New York: Crossroad, 1989), 224.

11. Quoted in Stephen Russell, *Overcoming Evil God's Way: The Biblical and Historical Case for Nonresistance* (Guys Mills, PA: Faithbuilders Resource Group, 2008), 99.

APPENDIX 1

1. Tim Reddish, PhD, MDiv, author of *Science and Christianity*, http://www.asamatteroffaith.com.

2. Rev. Dr. George Hermanson, United Church of Canada, co-director of the Madawaska Institute for Culture and Religion, Burnstown, ON.

3. R. Anderson Campbell, co-author of *Praying for Justice: A Lectionary of Christian Concern,* prayer given on September 14, 2014 at Theophilus Church, Portland, OR.

4. Donna Fiser Ward, pastor at Lighthouse United Methodist Church, Elizabeth, IN.

5. Brian McLaren, author of *The Great Spiritual Migration,* http://www.brianmclaren.net

6. Chuck McKnight, blogger at *Patheos,* http://www.HippieHeretic.com

7. Janyne McConnaughey, Ph.D., http://www.Janyne.org

8. Tim Reddish, PhD, MDiv, author of *Science and Christianity*, http://www.asamatteroffaith.com.

9. Bruce Epperly, author and co-author of over forty books, including *Praying with Process Theology: Spiritual Practices for Personal and Planetary Healing.*

10. Bruce Epperly.

11. Donna Fiser Ward, pastor at Lighthouse United Methodist Church, Elizabeth, IN.

12. Mark Karris, author of *Healing Heartbreak: Healing for the Heart, Brain, and Soul.* http://www.MarkGregoryKarris.com

13. L. Michaels, author of *Flip Flops, Glitter, and Theology,* http://www.flipflopsglitterandtheology.com

14. Rev. Dr. Tanya Linn Bennett, association dean for vocation and formation, Drew Theological School.

15. James Danaher, author of *Contemplative Prayer: A Theology for the 21st Century,* http://www.jamespdanaher.com.

16. Parker Loesch.

17. Dr. Dyton Owen, United Methodist pastor, writer, clergy coach, and author of *Jesus: God Revealed.*

18. Dr. Laurel Kearns, Associate Professor of Sociology of Religion and Environmental Studies at Drew Theological School.

19. Douglas S. Hardy, Nazarene Theological Seminary.

APPENDIX 2

1. Thomas Jay Oord, author of *The Uncontrolling Love of God* and many other books.

2. Glenn Siepert, blogger, podcast, and coach, http://www.MorningEncouragement.com.

3. Dr. Jay McDaniel, Professor of Religion, Hendrix College, and author of *Earth, Sky, Gods and Mortals: Developing an Ecological Spirituality.*

4. Dr. Heather Murray Elkins, Professor of Worship, Preaching, and the Arts, Drew Theological School.

5. Tim Reddish, PhD, MDiv, author of *Science and Christianity,* http://www.asamatteroffaith.com.

APPENDIX 3

1. Rev. Dr. George Hermanson, United Church of Canada, co-director of the Madawaska Institute for Culture and Religion, Burnstown, ON.

2. Eric Valosin, creative, artist, lay theologian, http://www.EricValosin.com.

3. Adapted from "A Prayer for the Easter Vigil," in Christopher Rodkey, Natalie Turri, and Jesse Turri, Coloring Lent: An Adult Coloring Book for the Journey to Resurrection (St. Louis: CBP/Chalice, 2017).

BIBLIOGRAPHY

Band, Chris. *On My Knees: Rebuilding Our Confidence in Prayer*. Oxford: Monarch Books, 2016.

Barth, Karl. *Church Dogmatics III.3: The Doctrine of Creation*. London: T&T Clark, 2004.

Basinger, David. "God Does Not Necessarily Respond to Prayer." Pages 255-263 in *Contemporary Debates in Philosophy of Religion*. Edited by Michael L. Peterson and Raymond J. VanArragon. Malden, MA: Blackwell, 2004.

Basinger, James W., and Paige A. Nunnelley. "Private Prayer Associations with Depression, Anxiety and Other Health Conditions: An Analytical Review of Clinical Studies." *Postgraduate Medicine* 28 (2016): 635–41.

Belt, Thomas G. *A Critical Evaluation of the Religious Adequacy of Open Theism: Toward an Open Theistic Theology of Petitionary Prayer*. MA diss., University of Wales, 2007.

Benson, Bruce Ellis, and Norman Wirzba. *The Phenomenology of Prayer*. New York: Fordham University Press, 2005.

Benson, Herbert, and Marg Stark. *Timeless Healing: The Power and Biology of Belief*. New York: Simon & Schuster, 1997.

Benson, Herbert, Jeffery A. Dusek, Jane B. Sherwood, Peter Lam, Charles F. Bethea, William Carpenter, Patricia L. Hibberd, et al. "Study of the Therapeutic Effects of Intercessory Prayer (STEP) in Cardiac Bypass Patients: A Multicenter Randomized Trial of Uncertainty and Certainty of Receiving Intercessory Prayer." *American Heart Journal* 5 (2006): 934–42. doi: 0.06/j.ahj.2005.05.028.

Bounds, Edward M. *Power Through Prayer*. Chicago: Moody, 2009.

Bounds, Edward M. *The Possibilities of Prayer*. New York: Fleming H. Revell, 1923.

Boyd, Gregory A. *Crucifixion of the Warrior God: Volumes 1 & 2*. Minneapolis: Augsburg Fortress, 2017.

Boyd, Gregory A. *God at War: The Bible & Spiritual Conflict*. Downers Grove, IL: InterVarsity Press, 1997.

Bruce, F. F. *The Book of the Acts*. Grand Rapids: Eerdmans, 1988.

Brueggemann, Walter. *Great Prayers of the Old Testament*. Louisville: Westminster John Knox, 2008.

Brümmer, Vincent. *What Are We Doing When We Pray? On Prayer and the Nature of Faith*. Farnham, Surrey, UK: Ashgate, 2008.

Buber, Martin. *I and Thou*. Translated by Walter Kaufmann. New York: Scribner's Sons, 1970.

Cacioppo, John T., and William Patrick. *Loneliness: Human Nature and the Need for Social Connection*. New York: Norton, 2008.

Cardy, Glynn. "A Progressive Christian Understanding of Prayer." Pages 133-148 in *Wisdom and Imagination: Religious Progressives and the Search for Meaning*. Edited by Rex A. E. Hunt and Gregory C. Jenks. Northcote, VIC: Morning Star, 2014.

Choi, Isaac. "Is Petitionary Prayer Superfluous?" Pages 32-62 in *Oxford Studies in Philosophy of Religion*, vol. 7. Edited by Jonathan Kvanvig. Oxford: Oxford University Press, 2016.

Claiborne, Shane, and Jonathan Wilson-Hartgrove. *Becoming the Answer to Our Prayers: Prayer for Ordinary Radicals*. Downers Grove, IL: InterVarsity Press, 2008.

Clements-Jewery, Philip. *Intercessory Prayer: Modern Theology, Biblical Teaching and Philosophical Thought*. Farnham, Surrey, UK: Ashgate, 2016.

Collins, John J. *The Apocalyptic Imagination: An Introduction to Jewish Apocalyptic Literature*. Grand Rapids: Eerdmans, 1998.

Collins, Raymond F. *The Power of Images in Paul*. Collegeville, MN: Liturgical Press, 2008.

Constable, Thomas L. *Talking to God: What the Bible Teaches about Prayer*. Grand Rapids: Baker Books, 1995.

Cook, Stephen L. *The Apocalyptic Literature*. Nashville: Abingdon, 2003.

Copan, Paul. *Loving Wisdom: Christian Philosophy of Religion*. Atlanta: Chalice, 2007.

Cozolino, Louis J. *The Neuroscience of Human Relationships: Attachment and the Developing Social Brain*. New York: Norton, 2006.

Crump, David. *Knocking on Heaven's Door: A New Testament Theology of Petitionary Prayer*. Grand Rapids: Baker Academic, 2006.

Davison, Scott A. *Petitionary Prayer: A Philosophical Investigation*. Oxford: Oxford University Press, 2017.

Duewel, Wesley L. *Mighty Prevailing Prayer: Experiencing the Power of Answered Prayer*. Grand Rapids: Zondervan, 1990.

Eisenberger, Naomi I., Matthew D. Lieberman, and Kipling D. Williams. "Does Rejection Hurt: An fMRI Study of Social Exclusion," *Science* 302 (2003): 290–92.

Epperly, Bruce. *Praying with Process Theology: Spiritual Practices for Personal and Planetary Healing*. Anoka, MN: River Lane Press, 2017.

Epperly, Bruce. *Process Theology: A Guide for the Perplexed*. London: T&T Clark, 2011.

Evans, Craig A. *The Bible Knowledge Background Commentary: Matthew–Luke*. Colorado Springs: Victor Books, 2003.

Evans, Tony. *Victory in Spiritual Warfare*. Eugene, OR: Harvest House, 2011.

Fiddes, Paul. *Participating in God: A Pastoral Doctrine of the Trinity*. London: Darton, Longman & Todd, 2000.

Fischer, Kathleen. *Reclaiming the Connections: A Contemporary Spirituality*. Kansas City: Sheed & Ward, 1990.

Foster, Charles. *The Sacred Journey*. Nashville: Nelson, 2010.

Frampton, Josian. *Pray and Watch the Impossible Happen*. Sarasota, FL: First Edition Design, 2014.

Gallagher, Robert L., and Paul Hertig, eds. *Mission in Acts: Ancient Narratives in Contemporary Context*. Maryknoll, NY: Orbis Books, 2004.

Gellman, Jerome. "Judaic Perspectives on Petitionary Prayer." Pages 129-148 in *Referring to God: Jewish and Christian Philosophical and Theological Perspectives*. Edited by Paul Helm. New York: Routledge, 2011.

Getz, Jack Corbin. *Praying When Prayer Doesn't Work: Finding A Way Back to the Heart of God.* Bloomington, IN: iUniverse, 2010.

Gundry, Robert H. *A Survey of the New Testament.* 5th ed. Grand Rapids: Zondervan, 2012.

Haas, Lauren. *A Philosophical Analysis of Petitionary Prayer.* PhD diss., Baylor University, 2012.

Hasker, William. *God, Time, and Knowledge.* Ithaca, NY: Cornell University Press, 1989.

Hasker, William. *The Triumph of God Over Evil: Theodicy for a World of Suffering.* Downers Grove, IL: InterVarsity Press, 2008.

Hodge, David R. "A Systematic Review of the Empirical Literature on Intercessory Prayer." *Research on Social Work Practice* 7 (2007). *ERIC*, EBSCO*host*.

Kalb, Claudia. "Don't Pray for Me! Please!" *Newsweek*, April 10, 2006.

Karris, Mark. "Rethinking the Phrase 'God Allowed.'" Pages 199-203 in *Uncontrolling Love: Essays Exploring the Love of God.* Edited by Chris Baker, Gloria Coffin, Craig Drurey, Graden Kirksey, Lisa Michaels, and Donna Fiser Ward. San Diego: SacraSage Press, 2017.

Karris, Mark. *Season of Heartbreak: Healing for the Heart, Brain, and Soul.* Grand Rapids: Kregel, 2017.

Koenig, Harold G. *Spirituality and Health Research: Methods, Measurements, Statistics, and Resources.* West Conshohocken, PA: Templeton Press, 2011.

Lewis, C. S., and Walter Hooper. *Christian Reflections.* Grand Rapids: Eerdmans, 1967.

MacBeth, Sybil. *Praying in Color: Drawing a New Path to God.* Brewster, MA: Paraclete Press, 2007.

Marshall, Ian Howard, *The Acts of the Apostles: An Introduction and Commentary.* Grand Rapids: Eerdmans, 1980.

Marty, Martin E. *Martin Luther: A Life.* New York: Viking, 2004.

Masters, Kevin S., Glen I. Spielmans, and Jason T. Goodson. "Are There Demonstrable Effects of Distant Intercessory Prayer? A Meta-Analytic Review." *Annals of Behavioral Medicine* 32 (2006): 21–26.

McGrath, Alister E. *Doubting: Growing Through the Uncertainties of Faith.* Downers Grove, IL: InterVarsity Press, 2006.

Mesle, C. Robert. *Process Theology: A Basic Introduction.* Atlanta: Chalice, 1993.

Moore, Kevin. *God, Conceivability, and Evil: The Logical Problem of Evil Revisited.* Crestwood, KY: Meta House, 2017.

Murray, Michael J. "God responds to Prayer." Pages 242-254 in *Contemporary Debates in Philosophy of Religion.* Edited by Michael L. Peterson and Raymond J. VanArragon. Malden, MA: Blackwell, 2004.

Newsom, Carol A., and Brennan W. Breed. *Daniel: A Commentary.* Louisville: Westminster John Knox, 2014.

Olver, Ian, and Andrew Dutney. "A randomized, blinded study of the impact of intercessory prayer on spiritual well-being in patients with cancer." *Alternative Therapies in Health and Medicine* 8 (2012): 8–27. doi: 0.007/978--464-457-5_5.

Oord, Thomas J. *The Nature of Love: A Theology.* Atlanta: Chalice, 2010.

Oord, Thomas J. *The Uncontrolling Love of God: An Open and Relational Account of Providence.* Downers Grove, IL: InterVarsity Press, 2016.

Origen. *Origen: An Exhortation to Martyrdom, Prayer, and Selected Works.* Translated by Rowan A. Greer. New York: Paulist, 1979.

Ortberg, John. *Faith & Doubt.* Grand Rapids: Zondervan, 2008.

Pak, Kenneth K. *Divine Power and Evil: A Reply to Process Theodicy.* London: Routledge, 2016.

Parish, Helen L., and William G. Naphy. *Religion and Superstition in Reformation Europe.* Manchester: Manchester University Press, 2002.

Pittenger, Norman. *The Holy Spirit.* Philadelphia: Pilgrim Press, 1974.

Plantinga, Cornelius, Jr. *Not the Way It's Supposed to Be: A Breviary of Sin.* Grand Rapids: Eerdmans, 1995.

Plummer, Robert L. *40 Questions About Interpreting the Bible.* Grand Rapids: Kregel, 2010.

Prince, Derek. *The Holy Spirit in You.* New Kensington, PA: Whitaker House, 1987.

Rees, Tomas James. "Is Personal Insecurity a Cause of Cross-National Differences in the Intensity of Religious Belief?" *Journal of Religion and Society* 11 (2009): 1–24.

Reichenbach, Bruce R. *Divine Providence: God's Love and Human Freedom.* Eugene, OR: Cascade Books, 2016.

Rey, Georges. "Meta-atheism: Religious Avowal as Self-Deception." Pages 243-265 in *Philosophers without Gods: Meditations on Atheism and the Secular Life.* Edited by Louise M. Anthony. Oxford: Oxford University Press, 2007.

Richards, Lawrence O. *The Bible Reader's Companion: Your Guide to Every Chapter of the Bible.* Colorado Springs: David C. Cook, 1991.

Rius-Camps, Josep, and Jenny Read-Heimerdinger. *The Message of Acts in Codex Bezae: A Comparison with the Alexandrian Tradition*, vol. 2. London: T&T Clark, 2004.

Rollins, Peter. *How (Not) to Speak of God.* Brewster, MA: Paraclete Press, 2006.

Russell, Stephen. *Overcoming Evil God's Way: The Biblical and Historical Case for Nonresistance.* Guys Mills, PA: Faithbuilders Resource Group, 2008.

Sartre, Jean-Paul. *Being and Nothingness.* New York: Pocket Books, 1984.

Sloan, Richard P. *Blind Faith: The Unholy Alliance of Religion and Medicine.* New York: St. Martin's Press, 2006.

Stott, John. *The Message of Acts: To the Ends of the Earth.* Leicester: Inter-Varsity Press, 1994.

Stott, John. *The Message of Romans: God's Good News for the World.* Downers Grove, IL: InterVarsity Press, 1994.

Strobel, Lee. *The Case for Christ: A Journalist's Personal Investigation of the Evidence for Jesus.* Grand Rapids: Zondervan, 1998.

Struve, Ann Riesselman, Der-Fa Lu, Laura Hart, and Theresa Keller. "The Use of Intercessory Prayer to Reduce Disruptive Behaviors of Patients with Dementia: A Pilot Feasibility Study." *Journal of Holistic Nursing* [serial online] 34 (2016): 35–45. doi: 0.77/0898005587400.

Suchocki, Marjorie. *God Christ Church: A Practical Guide to Process Theology.* New York: Crossroad, 1989.

Suchocki, Marjorie. *In God's Presence: Theological Reflections on Prayer.* Atlanta: Chalice, 1996.

Sweet, Leonard, and Frank Viola. *Jesus Speaks: Learning to Recognize and Respond to the Lord's Voice.* Nashville: W. Publishing Group, 2016.

Sweet, Leonard. *Nudge: Awakening Each Other to the God Who's Already There.* Colorado Springs: David C. Cook, 2010.

Sweet, Leonard. *So Beautiful: Divine Design for Life and the Church.* Colorado Springs: David C. Cook, 2009.

Thurman, Howard. *Essential Writings.* Edited by Luther E. Smith, Jr. Maryknoll, NY: Orbis Books, 2006.

Vardy, Peter, and Charlotte Vardy. *God Matters.* London: SCM, 2013.

Weaver, John B. *Plots of Epiphany: Prison-escape in Acts of the Apostles.* Berlin: de Gruyter, 2004.

Willard, Dallas. *The Divine Conspiracy.* London: William Collins, 1998.

Williamson, Samuel C. *Hearing God in Conversation: How to Recognize His Voice Everywhere.* Grand Rapids: Kregel, 2016.

Winkel, Stephanie, John Black, Patrick Pössel, Benjamin D. Jeppsen, Annie C. Bjerg, and Don T. Wooldridge. "Disclosure During Private Prayer as a Mediator Between Prayer Type and Mental Health in an Adult Christian Sample." *Journal of Religion and Health* 54 (2015): 540–53.

Wright, N. T. *The Day the Revolution Began: Reconsidering the Meaning of Jesus's Crucifixion.* San Francisco: HarperOne, 2016.

Yancey, Philip. *Prayer: Does it Make any Difference?* London: Hodder & Stoughton, 2006.

Yarbrough, Robert W. *1–3 John.* Grand Rapids: Baker Academic, 2008.

Young, William Paul. *The Shack: Where Tragedy Confronts Eternity.* Newbury Park, CA: Windblown Media, 2007.

Zaleski, Philip, and Carol Zaleski. *Prayer: A History.* Boston: Houghton Mifflin, 2005.

For more information about Mark Gregory Karris
or to contact him for speaking engagements,
please visit *www.markgregorykarris.com*

QUOIR

Many voices. One message.

Quoir is a boutique publishing company
with a single message: Christ is all.
Our books explore both His
cosmic nature and corporate expression.

For more information, please visit
www.quoir.com

CPSIA information can be obtained
at www.ICGtesting.com
Printed in the USA
LVHW081814030820
662257LV00032B/2154